C000158056

Micah Study Guide

Micah

STUDY GUIDE

Reg Carr

The Christadelphian
404 Shaftmoor Lane, Hall Green, Birmingham B28 8SZ, UK

©2010 The Christadelphian Magazine & Publishing Association Limited

First published 2010
ISBN 978 0 85189 189 7

Cover photograph:
A flock of sheep and goats in Syria
(Photograph © Koen Dantuma; source: www.sxc.hu. Used with permission)

Printed and bound in Malta by:
Gutenberg Press Ltd.

Contents

What is a Study Guide?

1 **Aims:** The overriding aim of all Bible study is that through knowledge and understanding of the word of God a person may become *"wise unto salvation through faith which is in Christ Jesus"* (2 Timothy 3:15).

"Study Guides" are designed to explain the straightforward teachings of scripture and where appropriate to emphasise:

a) First principles of doctrine

b) Practical outcomes

They should be helpful to young people, to those who are "young in the faith", who often have very little background knowledge of the scriptures, and to those of all ages and experience who enjoy straightforward, uncomplicated study of the Bible.

2 **Other features of Study Guides**

a) **Layout:** After a brief introduction to the book, essential background information is provided before looking at the text in more detail. Headings and verse references make it easy to use the guide for looking up information on any section of the Bible text.

b) **Bible versions:** This Guide mainly uses the New King James Version as a basis, as this helps to overcome problems of archaic expressions that exist in the Authorised (King James) Version (AV / KJV), which remains the most used translation in Christadelphian ecclesias today. Other versions can sometimes assist in clarifying a particular passage, but some popular modern versions are unreliable and betray the doctrinal bias of their translators.

c) **Manageable sections:** Each Guide is divided into units of study which are not too long. This will make it easier for individuals or groups to make progress. An hour's concentrated and productive study on a regular basis is likely to yield good results.

d) **Visual help:** The prophets and the Lord Jesus himself used visual illustrations to communicate their message. While the prime emphasis is on the written word, visual help is given wherever possible to increase understanding.

e) **Use alongside the Bible:** The student must have a Bible open alongside the Guide.

It is recommended at the outset that important information is marked in the Bible. Have a pencil at the ready.

f) **Further study:** The final sections contain suggestions for further study and a book list chosen on the basis of sound expositional and doctrinal content.

g) **Prayer:** We are studying the word of God. Before commencing any Bible study we must ask God's blessing on our activity. Thank God for making the Bible available to us, so that through it we may come to know Him and to look forward to His coming kingdom.

Here is a prayer that sums up our aim:

"Open thou mine eyes, that I may behold wondrous things out of thy law."
(Psalm 119:18)

Preface

THE short, but hard-hitting, prophecy of Micah has long been a favourite of mine, not simply because the prophet's work is set in such a crucial period of Israel's history, but also because the inspired words of Micah contain so much of value for our lives in Christ today.

Micah's words are full of what the Apostle Peter called *"the Spirit of Christ"* (1 Peter 1:11). There are not only many foretastes of the life and work of the Lord Jesus, but the prophecy itself also breathes many of the Lord's own personal characteristics – his fearless criticism of false shepherds, his tenderness towards the poor and needy, his zeal for the work of the Lord, his prayerfulness, his humility in the presence of God, his love of justice and of Divine righteousness.

All these things are valuable reminders to us of what it is that our God still requires of us, almost three millennia after Micah first delivered those memorable words:

> *"He has shown you, O man, what is good; and what does the LORD require of you but to do justly, to love mercy, and to walk humbly with your God?"*
>
> (Micah 6:8)

May the Lord bless us all in learning to appreciate the lessons of Micah's prophecy, to the end that much more of the Spirit of Christ may be found in the earth when the Messiah comes to rule as the Great Shepherd of his sheep, as the prophet Micah foresaw so long ago.

REG CARR
TUTBURY
June 2010

Acknowledgments

The publishers express their gratitude for the following illustrations:

- The photo of the Taylor Prism (page 7) – Roger Long.
- The illustration of Jerusalem (page 9) – Leen Ritmeyer.
- All maps – Mark Norris.
- All other illustrations are from copyright-free sources.

Introduction

AS readers of the prophecy of Micah we are comfortably introduced to the man of God by a summary of his credentials and origin, and a chronology of his ministry:

"The word of the LORD that came to Micah of Moresheth in the days of Jotham, Ahaz, and Hezekiah ... which he saw concerning Samaria and Jerusalem." (1:1)

But for Micah's contemporaries the introduction to the prophet would be sudden, without ceremony, and by the challenging cry of an open-air orator claiming to speak with divine authority:

"Hear, all you peoples! Listen, O earth, and all that is in it! Let the Lord GOD be a witness against you ..." (1:2)

The falling away of Judah at the end of Jotham's reign (2 Kings 15:35-37), and the descent of the nation into the depths of wickedness under Ahaz, who *"walked in the way of the kings of Israel"* (2 Kings 16:3), were the signal for God to move, by the power of the Holy Spirit, this unknown man from Moresheth Gath whose very name advertised the challenge implicit in his claims to speak for God: **Micah** – "Who is like Yah?". Just on its own, Micah's name was a reminder to all who heard his message that there was no God like the God of Israel, and that they were all guilty of failing to follow God's ways properly. So as Micah roamed from town to town, and as his name passed from tongue to tongue, it would serve to sharpen people's awareness that God had sent a prophet whose very name was a witness to the God who was also saying through the contemporary prophet Isaiah, *"I am God, and **there is none like me"*** (Isaiah 46:9).

Micah played on the meaning of his name so that his message might sink into ears that were not particularly attentive to the words of God. *"Who is a God like you?"*, the prophet asked (7:18), picking up a phrase from the song of victory that Moses had sung during the Exodus from Egypt many centuries earlier (Exodus 15:11). The phrase became almost a personal catchphrase for the prophet – a 'keyword memorial' of God's supremacy and of His power both to destroy the wicked and to save the righteous. So it was Micah's task to make Judah face up to that all-important choice: would they repent and turn again to serve their God as in the days of old, or would they continue in their wrongdoings and face the certainty of God's justifiable anger in judgement?

Many of the prophets of God were inspired to give hard-hitting messages designed to shake God's people from their lethargy. But there were few more challenging utterances than those which came from the lips of Micah. If you read the prophecies out loud, you can gain some idea of the powerful impact that the living prophet must have had on his contemporaries. Exclamations and questions abound in Micah's prophecies. Chapter 2:7 is a good example. Three quick questions were asked in a row, and the hearers were given no time to draw breath or to answer. The opening passage of chapter 3 is typical of Micah's assertive manner, which can perhaps be best compared to the way Jesus denounced the scribes and Pharisees in Matthew 23. Threats and warnings of destruction tumbled freely from Micah's lips, and the prophet justified his uncompromising approach by referring to his divine commission, which marked him out from the smooth-talking prophets of falsehood against whose lies he had to shout to be heard (2:6).

Micah's fiercest criticisms were reserved for the leaders of the nation, who were guilty of serial injustice, and were abusing their positions of power to accumulate wealth at the expense of the ordinary people. For this reason, Micah has often been thought of as the prophet of the poor and humble. It's certainly true that Micah moved in lower social circles than his contemporary Isaiah, who lived in Jerusalem and who was almost certainly on first-name terms with the princes of the realm. Like Bethlehem, Micah's home town of Moresheth Gath was "*little among the thousands of Judah*" (5:2). There was nothing noble about his birthplace in the foothills of the Shephelah, about 25 miles to the south-west of Jerusalem, and Micah's father does not even rate a mention.

And yet: just as the Lord Jesus Christ was to rise out of the comparative obscurity of Bethlehem to become the "*Ruler in Israel*", as Micah prophesied (5:2), so Micah himself was to undertake a prophetic ministry that grew to embrace both national doom and national salvation. Micah may be thought of as a 'minor' prophet because of the comparative shortness of his book; but his contemporary influence was very great indeed. It was Micah's words (rather than Isaiah's) which brought about the repentance and reformation under Hezekiah; and even a century after his death, it was Micah's powerful words that were able to save Jeremiah from otherwise certain death (Jeremiah 26:17-19).

A prophet of 'doom and gloom' Micah undoubtedly was. And yet those who listened to him with an attentive ear in the eighth century BC heard many comforting and reassuring words about the future that God always has in store for those who respond to Him in faith. So we shall look at Micah's message more closely in its personal, historical and prophetic light, to kindle that hope which is held out to every generation by this faithful prophet of God who "*being dead still speaks*" (Hebrews 11:4).

The kingdoms of Israel & Judah

IN THE SECOND HALF OF THE EIGHTH CENTURY BC

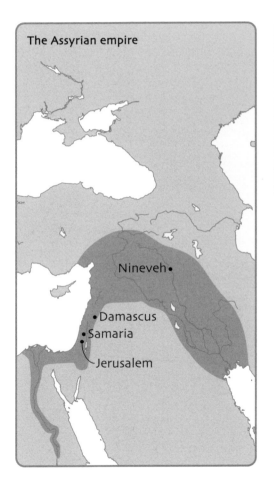

The Assyrian empire

> "For if one would understand the prophecies, it is necessary that one know how things were in the land, how matters lay, what was in the mind of the people – what plans they had with respect to their neighbours, friends and enemies – and especially what attitude they took in their country toward God and toward the prophet, whether they held to his word and worship or to idolatry."
> (Martin Luther)

THE most powerful political presence from the middle of the eighth century BC onwards was that of the Assyrian empire. For almost a century, Assyria's expansion had been resisted by a confederacy of nations (including the northern tribes of Israel); but with the accession of the warlike and dynamic Tiglath-pileser III in 745 BC, the Assyrians grew quickly in power, and began to expand their empire from their northern base in Nineveh (near modern-day Mosul, in Iraq). For almost the next 100 years, the threat of the warlike Assyrians was to loom large over the weaker nations of the ancient Near East.

The military expansion of Assyria under Tiglath-pileser III was at first resisted by Pekah, king of Israel, in alliance with the Syrians. Judah, on the other hand, under Ahaz, chose to appease the Assyrians by paying tribute to them (in spite of the warnings of the prophet Isaiah not to be afraid of all this military activity – Isaiah 8). The aggressive Assyrians, however, could not long be kept at bay, and events took a disastrous turn as the Assyrians set their eyes on the biggest prize of them all – Egypt.

In 732 BC, Damascus was conquered, and Syria was turned into an Assyrian province. Then Israel was attacked, and large portions of the northern kingdom were annexed by Tiglath-pileser. 2 Kings 15:29 recounts how *"Hazor, Gilead and Galilee, all the land of Naphtali"* were lost, and how the inhabitants of those places were carried away captive to Assyria. With his territory reduced to the small mountainous area around Samaria, the disgraced king of Israel, Pekah, was murdered and replaced by a puppet-king, Hoshea, who readily paid tribute money to the Assyrians.

When Shalmaneser V became king of Assyria around 727 BC, Hoshea decided to stop paying his annual tribute and made a league with Egypt instead. It was a serious mistake, as 2 Kings 17 records:

> "In the ninth year of Hoshea, the king of Assyria took Samaria and carried Israel away to Assyria, and placed them in Halah and by the Habor, the River of Gozan, and in the cities of the Medes."
> (verse 6)

The fall of Samaria (721 BC), after a siege lasting three years, was completed by Sargon II, almost immediately after his accession to the Assyrian throne (during the campaign Shalmaneser died unexpectedly). Sargon later boasted, in his official annals:

> "In the first year of my reign I besieged and conquered Samaria ... I led away 27,290 people who lived there."

The fall of Samaria, and the Assyrian captivity of its population, spelled the inglorious end of the northern kingdom of Israel. It had lasted just 250 years from the time it broke away from Judah during the reign of Rehoboam, Solomon's unwise son (1 Kings 12:19,20). Not one of Israel's kings had served the God of Israel faithfully, and the violent end of the kingdom had been foretold by a succession of prophets, one of the last of whom was Micah the Morasthite, whose ministry began during the reign of Jotham, and whose first recorded prophecy was directed against Samaria. Little Judah, with its hilltop capital Jerusalem, was left isolated and exposed, representing all that was left of the extensive empire of David and Solomon, which had once stretched all the way from the Euphrates in the north to the 'river of Egypt' in the south.

The prophet Micah, whose ministry covered at least part of the period from Jotham's accession (758 BC) to Hezekiah's death (697 BC), was a witness of all these historical events, and his prophecy cannot be properly understood without taking this background into account. Looking first at the real-life situations in which Micah's prophecies were spoken will help us a great deal in interpreting their fullest meaning.

The reign of Jotham (757-742 BC)

From the records in 2 Kings 15 and 2 Chronicles 26-27, we can piece together quite a full picture of Jotham's reign and character. He inherited the throne of Judah from his father Uzziah (Azariah), and his mother Jerushah was the daughter of a priest. Because of Uzziah's leprosy, Jotham served for a time as a kind of regent (2 Chronicles 26:21 – "Jotham ... was over the king's house, judging the people of the land").

Jotham was 25 years old when he became king in his own right, and he reigned for sixteen years over Judah. At the time of his accession, the northern kingdom of Israel, with Pekah as its usurper king, still had about 35 years left before its destruction by the Assyrians, and Syria still had about 15 years before Damascus fell to Tiglath-pileser.

Jotham built the upper gate of the temple in Jerusalem, and he also extended the "wall of Ophel". He fought wars against Pekah, against Rezin, king of Syria, and against the Ammonites, over whom he obtained a comprehensive victory, resulting in an annual tribute of 100 talents of silver, and 10,000 *"kors"* of both wheat and barley.* He is described in Chronicles as a *"mighty"* king, who *"prepared his ways before the LORD his God"*, and the record in 2 Kings 15:34 confirms this by saying that Jotham *"did what was right in the sight of the LORD; he did according to all that his father Uzziah had done"*.

Building on the prosperity and stability of his father Uzziah's reign, Jotham was a successful ruler from a human point of view. But all was not entirely well during his rule:

- There was **wickedness** in Judah. In spite of the relatively good personal example of the king, *"still the people acted corruptly"* (2 Chronicles 27:2).
- There was **self-indulgence and self-reliance** in Judah. Years of comparative prosperity had made the people materialistic and forgetful of God: they were living mostly for the present, largely unconcerned about the future. As Moses had warned the nation many centuries before (Deuteronomy 8:11-17), their prosperity had led to pride in their own achievements, at the expense of their devotion to God. And, as a direct result:

* A kor is a large measure equal to about 6 bushels or 220 litres.

- There was **idolatry** in Judah: *"... the high places were not removed; the people still sacrificed and burned incense on the high places"* (2 Kings 15:35).

It was towards the end of Jotham's reign, and in this worsening environment, that Micah began to speak the word of God in an effort to get his people to turn back to God before it was too late.

The reign of Ahaz (742-727 BC)

If all was not well in spiritual terms in Judah by the end of Jotham's comparatively good reign, things sank to a very much lower level under Ahaz, whose wickedness was to become legendary (*"This is that King Ahaz"*, says 2 Chronicles 28:22 disapprovingly). Taken together, the records in 2 Kings 16 and 2 Chronicles 28 paint a sorry picture of Ahaz's terrible personal example, which can be summarised as follows:

- He *"walked in the ways of the kings of Israel"* (2 Chronicles 28:2) rather than in the right ways of his father and grandfather (and we shall see from Micah's prophecy that this was one of God's principal complaints against the people of Judah).
- He personally **practised idolatry,** worshipping images of Baal, burning incense in the Valley of the Son of Hinnom (outside Jerusalem), sacrificing his children in the fire to Molech, and pursuing all sorts of idolatrous practices *"on the high places, on the hills, and under every green tree"* (2 Chronicles

28:4). He even caused idolatry to spread throughout his kingdom by building high places *"in every single city of Judah"* (verse 25).

- He **desecrated the temple** in Jerusalem: he replaced Solomon's bronze altar with a copy of a Syrian altar he had seen in Damascus (in the vain hope that the gods of Syria might help him!); he interfered with the temple's furniture and fittings and stripped it of much of its silver and gold in order to buy the protection of the Assyrians against Israel and Syria; and he closed up the private royal entrance to the temple, simply to please the king of Assyria.

- He **refused God's help** against the warlike confederacy of Israel and Syria (Isaiah 7), and instead made a submissive alliance with Assyria, which turned out to be an untrustworthy ally: Tiglath-pileser *"came to (Ahaz) and distressed him, and did not assist him"* (2 Chronicles 28:20). And as a direct result of all this wickedness:

- *"**The Lord brought Judah low because of Ahaz** king of Israel"* (2 Chronicles 28:19), and especially by bringing up multiple enemies against them.

The Chronicler's summary of the reign of Ahaz could hardly be more critical: "*... he had encouraged moral decline in Judah and had been continually unfaithful to the* LORD" (2 Chronicles 28:19). The corruption and injustice that Micah found in Judah, the harsh and selfish oppression of the poor, and the general breakdown of society, were all the outcome of the dreadful example set by this most wicked king.

Hezekiah's reign (727-697 BC)

There could hardly have been a greater contrast between two kings than there was between Ahaz and his son Hezekiah. From the earliest days of his sole rulership (there is some evidence that he may have been co-regent with Ahaz for at least a few years), Hezekiah set about reforming the things that his father had spoiled so badly:

- In the very first month of his reign, he **began to repair the temple**, rededicating it to the worship of God (2 Chronicles 29).

- In the second month, he **reinstituted the Passover feast** in Jerusalem (2 Chronicles 30).

- He **destroyed all the graven images**, high places and altars to false idols that his father had built (2 Chronicles 31:1).

- He **re-established the Mosaic system of tithes** and freewill offerings for the work of the Levites in the House of God (2 Chronicles 31:4-12).

- He **refused to join the Philistines and the Egyptians** in rebelling against the Assyrians, relying on God instead, taking advice from God's true prophets, Isaiah and Micah, while at the same time strengthening the defences and the water supply of Jerusalem, and being rewarded by a miraculous deliverance from the invading army of Sennacherib (2 Chronicles 32:20-22).

- When struck down with a terminal disease, he **prayed earnestly to God and was given an extension of life** (2 Chronicles 32:24-26 and Isaiah 38).

- He **brought back many of the refugees and captives** who had been displaced by the Assyrians, and he was *"exalted in the sight of all nations"* (2 Chronicles 32:23), inaugurating a brief golden age of peace and prosperity (there was *"peace and truth"* in his days – Isaiah 39:8) which served as a foretaste of the eternal kingdom of God on earth.

- Because he **consistently sought the Lord**, and *"did it with all his heart"*, he *"prospered"* in all that he did (2 Chronicles 31:21), and God deferred the threatened destruction of Jerusalem out of regard for him (2 Chronicles 32:26).

Hezekiah's reign was the best of times, not only for Judah and the people of God, but also for Micah as God's mouthpiece. Having laboured in vain to be heard during the reigns of Jotham and Ahaz, Micah was able to end his ministry on a rewarding note thanks to the responsiveness of Hezekiah to the word of God.

Hezekiah was a ruler whose life spoke of even better things to come *"in the latter days"*. The comforting long-term glimpses of Messiah that Micah saw (2:13; 5:2,4,5; 7:1-7) were given real-life substance in the person of the godly Hezekiah; and beyond all the difficulties of the eighth century BC, Micah and the faithful were able to see the glorious restoration that still lies ahead for the people of God.

Sennacherib and Hezekiah: The Taylor Prism

After being turned back from his Judean campaign in 701 BC, Sennacherib recorded the Taylor Prism, which is currently in the British Museum, London (another version is preserved in the Oriental Institute Museum of Chicago). It is inscribed as follows: "As for the king of Judah, Hezekiah, who had not submitted to my authority, I besieged and captured forty-six of his fortified cities, along with many smaller towns, taken in battle with my battering rams … I took as plunder 200,150 people, both small and great, male and female, along with a great number of animals including horses, mules, donkeys, camels, oxen, and sheep. As for Hezekiah, I shut him up like a caged bird in his royal city of Jerusalem. I then constructed a series of fortresses around him, and I did not allow anyone to come out of the city gates. His towns which I captured I gave to the kings of Ashdod, Ekron, and Gaza."

Amazingly in this account, Sennacherib admits he never captured Hezekiah or the city of Jerusalem, even though he sent a large army against it …

A chronological chart
summarising the key events in the period during which Micah prophesied:

Year BC	Place / country	Event(s)
758	Israel	Accession of Pekah
757	Judah	Accession of Jotham
745	Assyria	Accession of Tiglath-pileser III (Pul)
742	Judah	Accession of Ahaz
735-732	Syria and Israel	The Syro-Ephraimite alliance against Assyria
732	Syria	Tiglath-pileser besieges and takes Damascus
730	Israel	Accession of Hoshea
727	Assyria; Judah	Accession of Shalmaneser V; Accession of Hezekiah
725-2	Israel	Hoshea rebels and Shalmaneser besieges Samaria
721	Assyria; Israel	Accession of Sargon; Fall of Samaria
719	Judah	Sargon's Shephelah campaign and victory over Egyptians and Philistines at Raphia (Gaza Strip)
714-713	Judah	Hezekiah's sickness and recovery
713-712	Judah; Philistia	Assyrian invasions of south-west Judah (Sargon and his son Sennacherib); Siege and fall of Ashdod
705	Assyria	Accession of Sennacherib
701	Judah	Sennacherib's invasion: army destroyed
697	Judah	Accession of Manasseh

Micah's message for his times

AN OVERVIEW

> "The true function of a prophet is not simply to announce calamities, but to lead the people to conversion."
>
> (J.I. Alfaro)

TRY to picture the scene. It's somewhere between the years 740 and 730 BC, and a new prophet has suddenly appeared in Judah's capital Jerusalem. He's from some obscure country town down in the south-west, and he's apparently been

disturbing the peace in and around his home with alarmist tales about destruction from the Lord. But even though Samaria and the northern tribes of Israel might eventually be overrun by the Assyrians, there's really no need for such defeatist talk in Judah. After all, this is Jerusalem! This is God's capital city, where He's chosen to dwell in His magnificent temple. We're as safe as houses here. God would never allow David's descendants to be removed from the throne of Judah. In any case, those northern tribes deserve everything they get: it was they who perversely chose to break away from God's holy city …

This was the state of complacency that Micah found in Jerusalem when he went up to Judah's capital in the reign of Ahaz, to continue the ministry which he had begun a few years earlier in the time of Jotham. The people of Judah were so lacking in self-awareness that Micah had to try to persuade them all the harder to recognise that they were behaving no better in their duty towards God than their northern counterparts. In Jerusalem itself, God could see every kind of disobedience to His laws, and He was determined either to reform it, through the work of His prophets,

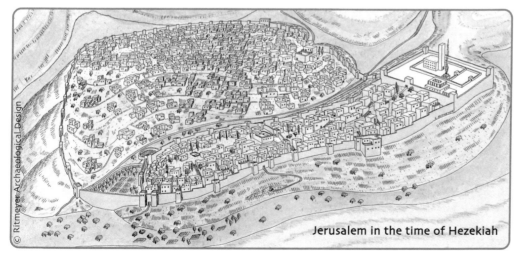

Jerusalem in the time of Hezekiah

or to purge it, by the destroying armies of foreign invaders.

When we bear in mind this wayward state of Israel and Judah in the early years of Micah's ministry, we can only marvel at the longsuffering of God, and see in the prophet's mission yet another evidence of God's mercy towards His erring people. King Jotham, in whose reign Micah first prophesied, received a personal commendation in the inspired record (2 Kings 15:34); and yet the king's influence on his people was virtually non-existent, with the high places of idolatry still present (verse 35). The displeasure of the Almighty towards these idolatrous practices showed itself in the military invasions by Judah's enemies at the end of Jotham's reign (verse 37); and that same Divine displeasure against the nation's idolatry was reflected in the language of Micah's first recorded prophecy: *"For behold, the* Lord *is coming out of his place; he will come down and tread on the* **high places** *of the earth"* (Micah 1:3).

The destruction of the northern kingdom of Israel would surely come if they did not soon repent; and, as an object lesson to Judah, Micah was inspired to foretell the details of Samaria's approaching doom (1:5-9). His message to Judah was equally clear: Samaria's "wounds" were incurable; and the Assyrians (*"the rod of my anger"* as God called them through Micah's contemporary, Isaiah – 10:5) would definitely bring Divine punishment on God's people. If Judah did not turn away from idolatry, that same

destroying army would be brought down south *"to the gate of my people, even to Jerusalem"* (1:9).

It's immediately apparent from the location of the towns and villages mentioned in Micah's opening prophecy (1:10-16) that this pronouncement of judgement to come was directed towards the area around Micah's home where his ministry almost certainly began. Like the Lord Jesus Christ (Matthew 11:20-24), Micah was given the unpleasant task of telling the people of his own region that their 'unrepentant' towns were doomed. Judgement was already on its way; and it was Micah's job to depict their coming fate as an eye-witness might describe an erupting volcano, ravaging and engulfing everything in its path (1:4).

Micah himself, of course, could take no pleasure in foretelling this violent fate for the people of his locality: like all God's prophets, he sympathised deeply with the sufferings that so many of his friends and neighbours were to experience. He was obviously upset by some of the awful things which he had to predict in the name of his God (1:8). And he was particularly distressed because the destruction of the northern tribes (foretold in 1:6,7, and fulfilled within a few years by Sargon) was destined to bring in its wake the invasion and desecration of the prophet's home town of Moresheth Gath (1:14).

Yet when Micah turned his attention to the inhabitants of Jerusalem (chapter 2

onwards), he found even greater wickedness at the heart of the capital city. It was full of corruption and oppression – it was being built up with bloodshed (3:10). Greedy landlords were seizing fields and houses that did not belong to them, driving out poor widows and their defenceless children. Justice was being perverted on every side; the traders were dishonest; the powerful were abusing their authority; the priests were forever taking bribes; and there were families in crisis all over the city, with sons and daughters disowning their parents and showing them no natural affection.

Like all the prophets, Micah spoke a message that was particularly meaningful for his times, so it's important to understand the historical context. But the prophets were neither journalists nor political analysts. They were commentators on the spiritual significance that contemporary events had for the personal lives of God's people, and they tried continually to remind their hearers that God was in control of the forces that were shaping the world in which they lived.

In another way also, Micah's message was typical of every other God-given prophecy: it was aimed at the heart and conscience, and was designed to awaken a sense of moral responsibility in every individual. Certain types of behaviour were (and still are) unacceptable to God, and the frequent occurrence of the word "therefore" in Micah's prophecy was a clear indication that wrong decisions and actions would bring inevitable consequences. But behind it all, the faithfulness of God to His promises persisted. And there was more than enough, entwined among Micah's pictures of coming doom, to keep alive the hope of restoration, of the coming of Messiah and of his everlasting kingdom of peace.

Micah's prophecies appear to have been organised into three parts by the prophet himself at the end of his ministry.* These three parts are, in effect, Micah's own 'edited highlights' of his long career as a prophet; and this structure provides us with a convenient framework for summarising Micah's message.

Part one (1:2 to 2:13):

Contains prophecies probably first delivered in the time of Jotham and Ahaz (757-727 BC). It begins with a solemn warning about God's coming judgements, and a description of an impressive vision of the Lord God descending to punish both Israel and Judah. Micah sees the northern capital Samaria destroyed, with the devastation reaching the gates of Jerusalem. The destructive advance of the Assyrian army across Judah's south-western foothills is depicted through an extended word-play on the names of the towns and villages around Micah's own birthplace. God is going to punish His people because of their corruption, greed, idolatry and violence. They have ignored

---

* See the note (in chapter 4) on the tell-tale phrase *"And I said"* in Micah 3:1.

God's previous threats because they were over-confident about their privileged position as the 'chosen people', and they reject any criticisms made by God's true prophets, preferring instead to listen to drunkards. The section ends with a short promise of subsequent restoration and deliverance.

Part two (3:1 to 5:15):

Contains prophecies possibly first delivered during the co-regency of Ahaz and Hezekiah (732-727 BC). It consists of three chapters, the first of which roundly condemns the leaders of Judah, while the other two are extended predictions of deliverance for Zion and of Divine vengeance on the nations around. Micah tells the rulers of Jerusalem forcefully that failure to mend their ways will bring about the destruction of the city. Yet beyond the punishment, he also holds out the distant prospect of a time when the reformed nation will serve as a beacon for God's law, and when the nations of the world will flock to Jerusalem for teaching and leadership in a time of universal peace. Despite the worries of the present time, Jerusalem will ultimately triumph over her enemies, through the work of a Shepherd-King from Bethlehem who will save God's people and cleanse the world of idolatry and war.

Part three (6:1 to 7:20):

Contains prophecies from the time of Hezekiah (727-697 BC). It follows the same basic pattern as the two other parts (with a 'judgement' section followed by a

'deliverance' section); but this time the judgement section is cast as a courtroom scene, in which God is the plaintiff (and the Judge), His people and the city of Jerusalem are the defendants, and Micah plays the part of the court usher, directing the proceedings and recording them. If the suggested dating of the prophecy is accurate (in 727 BC, just as Hezekiah became sole ruler of Judah), then it becomes possible to see the young Hezekiah as the "man" who speaks on behalf of God's people (6:8). Seen in that same light, Hezekiah's personal sorrow at the judgements pronounced by God on Judah and Jerusalem is almost certainly reflected in these chapters, and the deliverance promised can be seen as having an initial fulfilment in the short 'golden age' under Hezekiah following the destruction of the Assyrian army. In any event, Micah makes it clear that the repentant children of God can always rely on Him to forgive them, and to restore their fortunes, as He promised faithfully in His covenant with the fathers of old.

The 'therefores' in Micah

The ominous 'therefores' of Micah's prophecies clearly demonstrate that there is a direct link between behaviour and consequence. Looked at together in this way, they illustrate very clearly that it was because of their sins against God that such catastrophic events engulfed the people of Israel and Judah in Micah's time and beyond.

Cause	Therefore	Effect
Israel's sin	1:6	Samaria to be ruined
Samaria's destruction	1:8	Micah's lamentations
Israel's sins found in Judah	1:14	Moresheth Gath to be 'given away' to the invader
Covetous and violent oppression in Judah	2:3	God devising disaster against them
Robbing of inheritances	2:5	Judah to have no inheritance
Prophets speaking lies	3:6	No visions to be given
Rulers hating justice	3:12	Jerusalem to be destroyed
Striking the judge of Israel on the cheek	5:3	God will 'give them up'
Dishonest trading; violence and lying	6:13	God will strike them and make them desolate
Israel's sins found in Judah	6:16	God's people to 'bear their reproach'
Nobody to be trusted	7:7	Only God can help

Micah's mission was to make God's people see that their wrongdoing, though it might go unpunished because of their ability to buy off their human judges, would not go unpunished by their God, the divine Judge.

Micah's prophecy

AT CLOSE QUARTERS

THE detail of Micah's prophecy can be more easily understood by breaking down the book's contents into the following three-part structure:

PART ONE (1:2 to 2:13):	PART TWO (3:1 to 5:15):	PART THREE (6:1 to 7:20):
"Hear, all you peoples!"	*"Hear now, O heads of Jacob"*	*"Hear now what the Lord says ... Hear, O you mountains"*
a) 1:2–2:11: JUDGEMENT on Israel and Judah	a) 3:1-12: JUDGEMENT on Judah's leaders	a) 6:1-7:10: JUDGEMENT on the people of Judah and the city of Jerusalem: the great assize court
1:2 Famous last words, famous first words	3:1-4 No justice from the rulers	6:1-5 Yahweh versus the people
1:3-7 Samaria, a heap of ruins	3:5-8 Misdeeds of the false prophets	6:6-8 Spokesman for the defence: What does God want?
1:8-16 A lament for the towns and villages of Judah	3:9-12 A false sense of security	6:9-12 Yahweh versus Jerusalem
2:1-11 "For this is an evil time"	b) 4:1-5:15: DELIVERANCE for Zion and vengeance on the nations	6:13-16 The sentence of the Judge
b) 2:12-13: DELIVERANCE for a remnant	4:1-5 The Lord's reign in Zion	7:1-10 The defendant's lament and confession
2:12 "Like a flock in the midst of their pasture"	4:6-8 Zion's time of triumph	b) 7:11-20: Ultimate DELIVERANCE for God's people
2:13 The "one who breaks open"	4:9-13 Zion's daughter: saved out of Babylon	7:11-13 Jerusalem rebuilt and repopulated
	5:1-6 The Ruler in Israel: Hezekiah and Christ	7:14-15 The prophet's prayer and the Divine response
	5:7-9 The roles of the rescued remnant	7:16-20 The nations humbled and God's promises fulfilled: "Who is like Yah?"
	5:10-15 Getting rid of worldliness	

Part one (1:2 to 2:13)

"HEAR, ALL YOU PEOPLES"

> **(A) 1:2 TO 2:11: JUDGEMENT ON ISRAEL AND JUDAH**

1:2 – Famous last words, famous first words

It's possible that the first thing that Micah's contemporaries would know about him would be the sound of the challenging words with which he began to shout for their attention: *"Hear, all you peoples!"* (1:2).

But these opening words of Micah's first stern message of warning about God's judgements to come were chosen by the prophet not simply to draw a crowd of hearers around him. In fact, Micah was deliberately quoting the last-recorded words of one of his prophetic predecessors. For these were the final words with which Micah's 'namesake' Micaiah, 150 years earlier, had chillingly foretold the violent death of wicked King Ahab: *"If you ever return in peace"*, Micaiah had said to Ahab, *"the LORD has not spoken by me ... Take heed, all you people(s)!"* (1 Kings 22:28). (Although Micaiah's words in 1 Kings 22:28 and Micah's in Micah 1:2 are translated differently in the English versions, they are identical in the Hebrew text. The same Hebrew word *(shamea)* is used for *"take heed"* and *"hear"*, and the Hebrew word for *"people"* is used in the plural in both cases.)

There were at least three reasons why Micah picked up these famous last words of a faithful prophet from an earlier time:

- Both prophets shared the same name: **Micah** is just a shortened form of **Micaiah**; so Micah was pointedly identifying himself with the earlier prophet in his denunciation of wickedness in high places.

- Micah was claiming for his own message the same Divine origin as that which had prompted Micaiah to say, in effect, with such great confidence: *'Just you mark my words, everybody!'*

- It was a pointer to the fact that both the southern and the northern kingdoms of Judah and Israel, 150 years after the excessively evil times of Ahab, had now fallen to those same moral and spiritual depths.

Micah was to make this parallel between his own days and the days of Micaiah even more explicit in a later prophecy: *"For the statutes of Omri are kept"*, said Micah, and "*all the works of Ahab's house are done; and you walk in their counsels*" (6:16).

All this, then, was contained in Micah's re-use of Micaiah's last words of inspired foreboding, and it was a highly effective place for his prophesyings to begin. Significantly, too, Micah was to make this the signature-tune for each of his separate prophecies, with a variation on Micaiah's words introducing each new part of the edited version of his own messages (see 3:1 and 6:1).

It seems likely also that, in calling on the "*earth*" to "*listen*" to the "*witness*" of the Lord God against His people (1:2), Micah was making a deliberate reference to the song in which Moses had called on "*the earth*" to "*hear*" his final prophecy, in words which would remain for ever as a "*witness*" against them whenever they strayed from following their God (Deuteronomy 31:21).

This reference to the Song of Moses was the first of many allusions by Micah to the Pentateuch (the five books of Moses). There are so many of these references in Micah's seven chapters that an earlier commentator has concluded: "It is plain that (Micah) had the writings (of Moses) before him and expected his hearers to recognise his allusions".* The panel on the opposite page listing some of Micah's references to the books of Moses illustrates

the extent to which it was part of Micah's mission – in common with all the true prophets – to try to bring about a revival of the religion taught by Moses during the Exodus. It was almost certainly because the Law of Moses was no longer generally respected that both Israel and Judah came to develop the kind of secular and commercial culture that Micah criticised so fiercely.

Micah's use of the word "*witness*" too, with the legal overtones which were certainly present in Deuteronomy 31:21, suggests that this first section of Micah's prophecy, like the third (6:1 onwards), was meant to be understood as a courtroom drama, with the Lord God testifying against His people and then delivering His judgement on them. (The Hebrew word *anah*, 'to testify', was in fact used by Moses in Deuteronomy 31:21 and by Micah later in his prophecy – 6:3.) And as Micah made clear, God was pronouncing judgement directly "*from his holy temple*", which King Jotham had neglected (2 Chronicles 27:2), and which Jotham's wicked son Ahaz had actually profaned (2 Kings 16:8-18).

1:3-7 – Samaria, a heap of ruins

Coming perhaps towards the end of Jotham's far-from-perfect reign (see 2 Kings 15:34,35), this first prophetic utterance of Micah may just have pre-dated the military

---

* Fred Pearce, *From Hosea to Zephaniah* (Birmingham, The Christadelphian, 1979), page 131.

References to the Books of Moses

Micah	Pentateuch	Allusion / reference
2:2	Exodus 20:17	"… you shall not covet …"
2:5	Deuteronomy 23:2	"the congregation of the Lord"
2:10	Deuteronomy 12:9,10	"… you have not come to the rest"
3:4	Deuteronomy 31:17,18	"I (God) will hide my face"
3:11	Deuteronomy 31:17	"God is not among us"
4:1	Deuteronomy 4:30	"… in the latter days"
5:12	Deuteronomy 18:10-12	Sorceries and soothsayers an abomination to the Lord
5:13	Deuteronomy 5:8; 16:22	Prohibitions against carved images and standing stones
6:2	Deuteronomy 32:1	"Hear, O earth"
6:4	Deuteronomy 7:8	"redeemed from the house of bondage (in Egypt)"
6:8	Deuteronomy 10:12,13	"What does the LORD your God require of you?"
6:10,11	Deuteronomy 25:13,14	"differing weights" "differing measures"
6:13-15	Deuteronomy 28:15-19	Punishments for disobedience
7:3	Deuteronomy 16:19	Taking bribes
7:6	Deuteronomy 32:15	Lack of respect and loyalty within the family
7:18	Exodus 15:11	"Who is like you, O LORD?"
7:18	Exodus 34:6,7	The character of God revealed to Moses
7:20	Genesis 22:16	God has "sworn" to bless Abraham and his descendants

inroads made into Judah by Syria and the northern tribes of Israel (2 Kings 15:37). But those inroads were themselves expressions of God's displeasure with Judah, and Micah made it clear from the outset of his ministry that Jerusalem would not necessarily be spared from the punishments that were soon to come down on the northern kingdom.

God Himself would supervise and direct the dramatic overthrow of Samaria, where idolatry and immorality had stretched God's patience to breaking point. And so Micah foretold Samaria's end, using the language of storm and cataclysm so familiar in the Psalms (Psalm 18:7-15 and 97:5) and Amos (especially Amos 4:13, where the context is also a prophecy against Samaria). Mountains melting, and valleys running down like molten wax (Micah 1:4) may be poetic images conveying the intensity of the fire of God's anger; but the awful reality of destruction at the hands of the cruel Assyrians would be felt as literally as a volcano or an earthquake when the Lord God came *"out of his place"* (verse 3) to *"tread on the high places"* (the very places where the kings of Israel had worshipped idols since the days of Jeroboam – 1 Kings 12:31).

Fulfilled by Sargon in 721 BC, these first recorded words of Micah were intended as an early warning to King Jotham and his son Ahaz that it would only be a matter of time before Judah's waywardness brought about the same fate for Jerusalem (verse 5). But in the meantime Samaria would become *"a heap of ruins in the field"*, and God would *"pour down her stones into the valley"* (verse 6) as a punishment for all the unfaithfulness the city and her people had shown in going after other gods (verse 7).

1:8-16 – A lament for the towns and villages of Judah

So Micah's first message was unmistakably clear: Samaria had *"incurable wounds"*. (The New King James Version is accurate in verse 9: the Hebrew text has the word for 'wound' in the plural.) There was no remedy for Israel; but what was important was the fact that, if Judah did not turn away from those same idols of wood and stone, then the Assyrian would also be brought down *"to the gate of ... Jerusalem"* (verse 9).

And in such an eventuality – which Micah depicted like a swift Assyrian chariot in verses 10 to 16 – it would not be just Jerusalem that suffered. The enemy invasion would sweep first through the maritime plain of the Philistines and up into the south-western foothills of Judah (the nation's 'soft underbelly'), with no town or village left unscathed. Micah's own home town, Moresheth Gath, was a fortified place in the very centre of those foothills; and it must have been one of the hardest tasks of the prophet's life to be the messenger of doom to so many of his fellow-countrymen, his neighbours and perhaps even his family. It was Micah's unhappy lot to have to describe, as an eye-witness before the event, the coming

Samaria – *"a heap of ruins in the field"*

"The stones of the temples and palaces of Samaria have been carefully removed from the rich soil, thrown together in heaps, built up in ... terraces, and rolled down into the valley below." (J. L. Porter, *Handbook for Travellers in Syria and Palestine*)

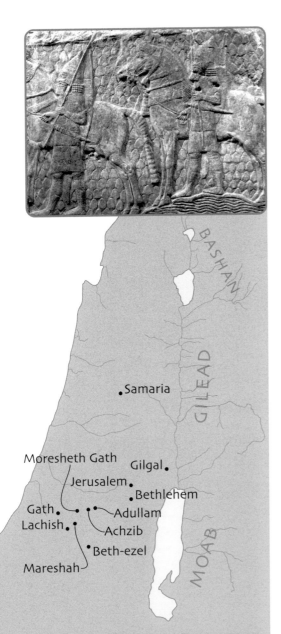

destruction of all the familiar places of his homeland.

Micah himself, like the Lord Jesus when he foretold the coming destruction of Jerusalem in later years (Matthew 23:37), was deeply distraught by the dreadful things he had to predict in the name of his God: *"Therefore I will wail and howl, I will go stripped and naked; I will make a wailing like the jackals and a mourning like the ostriches"* (1:8).For some reason, we all know that jackals 'howl'; but we seem less aware that the ostrich is capable of making what have been described as *"gruesome groans"*. And for Micah to *"go stripped and naked"*, as a sign of defeat and humiliation, shows how very much he entered into the sufferings of those who were going to be caught up in the coming foreign invasions. Like Ezekiel when he acted out the siege and fall of Jerusalem (Ezekiel 4 and 5), Micah must have presented a curious appearance to any onlookers who saw him playing the part of a 'man of sign' in this dramatic way.

From the point of view of military history, verses 10 to 15 of this first prophecy of Micah are really fascinating. The Shephelah (or Lowland) district was an important area from a strategic point of view. It commanded access to the Judean highlands, and it served many invading forces as a convenient 'back door' through which to attack the nation's capital. While some northern invaders (like Nebuchadnezzar, for example) preferred to come at Jerusalem from the north, the Assyrians chose to approach Jerusalem from the south-west, and the villages mentioned in Micah appear to have been attacked and overrun several times. Not even Hezekiah's wonderful prayer to God (2 Kings 19:15-19), which God answered by turning Sennacherib's army away from the gates of Jerusalem, was able to save the villages of the Shephelah from the northern invaders. Hence Micah's soulful lament over their predicted doom.

It was undoubtedly in a systematic attempt to make Micah's message memorable to those who first heard it, rather than out of a macabre sense of humour, that the Spirit, through Micah, resorted to playing skilfully on the names of the Judean towns and villages which would be caught up in any invasion which approached Jerusalem from the south-west. It is not easy to identify with certainty some of the smaller places whose names are recorded by Micah in these verses; and several of the meanings are not as clear to us as they must have been to Micah and his contemporaries. But the overall point is obvious: the Assyrian army would slice through the foothills of Judah, in a destructive sweep which would reach right to the gates of Jerusalem. A 25-mile-wide corridor of land would be full of weeping as the Assyrian war-machine rolled all the way from Gath up to Jerusalem.

We can reconstruct this trail of Assyrian destruction by following the story as Micah describes it through a series of puns, or plays-on-words:

- **1:10** – *"Tell it not in Gath"*: David used these same words in mourning the deaths of Saul and Jonathan (2 Samuel 1:20). By Micah's time, the saying had perhaps become proverbial. Like David before him, Micah didn't want the Philistines to rejoice at the misery of God's people.

- **1:10** – *"... in Beth Aphrah, roll yourself in the dust"*: Beth Aphrah means 'House of Dust'.

- **1:11** – *"Pass by in naked shame, you inhabitant of Shaphir"*: Shaphir means 'beauty'. The villagers from 'Beauty town' would be stripped bare and taken into captivity looking anything but beautiful.

- **1:11** – *"The inhabitant of Zaanan does not go out"*: Zaanan means 'marching', but the Assyrian invasion would make sure there was nowhere safe for them to march.

- **1:11** – *"Beth Ezel mourns; its place to stand is taken away"*: the town's name means 'taking away'.

- **1:12** – *"For the inhabitant of Maroth pined for good, but disaster came down from the LORD ..."*: Maroth means 'bitterness' – the very opposite of what the townspeople wanted.

- **1:13** – *"O inhabitant of Lachish, harness the chariot to the swift steeds"*: Lachish means 'horse', like the horses which would bring Assyrian destruction to the town. Micah also

Lachish – *"the beginning of sin"* to Jerusalem (Micah 1:13)

Lachish was an important border-town in the foothills of the Shephelah, 30 miles south-west of Jerusalem, and only four or five miles from Micah's own home town. It was conquered by Joshua, who assigned it to the tribe of Judah (Joshua 10:32; 15:39). In later years it stood right on the border of Philistine territory, and was very close to the coast road along which the armies of Africa and Asia always travelled in search of conquest.

At the time of Micah it was a key strategic target for armies invading Judah and would be very vulnerable to attack. The Assyrians took Lachish during several campaigns in and around Judah (in 719, 711 and 701 BC); and it was from there that Sennacherib sent his emissaries to Jerusalem to intimidate Hezekiah (2 Kings 18:14-17). Although there are quite a few references to Lachish in scripture, and especially to its status as a well-defended garrison city, Micah 1:13 is the only place where we are told that it 'started the spiritual decline' in Judah, most likely by being the first city to import idolatrous practices from the northern kingdom. Some commentators, however, understand the phrase *"the beginning of sin"* in Micah 1:13 to refer to Lachish's over-reliance on the horses and chariots of Egypt (see also Micah 5:10).

accused Lachish of being *"the beginning of sin to the daughter of Zion"* – meaning perhaps that Lachish was the place where the idolatry practised in Israel first found a foothold in Judah.

- **1:14** – *"... you shall give presents to Moresheth Gath"*: Moresheth means 'possession'. The 'presents' would consist of Micah's home town, which would be part of the 'dowry', or bridal presents, that the daughter of Zion (i.e. Jerusalem, mentioned in verse 13) would have to give to the invader: *"Zion is to say farewell to Moresheth-gath, as to a bride who is lost to her family".**

- **1:14** – *"The houses of **Achzib** shall be a lie":* a play on the Hebrew word *achzab,* meaning a winter brook that dries up in the summer, disappointing the thirsty traveller.
- **1:15** – *"I will yet bring an heir to you, O inhabitant of **Mareshah**":* Mareshah means 'inheritance'. The inheritance would be lost and the heir (the new owner) would be a foreign invader. (Mareshah had been a key part of Rehoboam's Judean defensive system, and it would be a valuable prize for the invading Assyrians – 2 Chronicles 11:5-12.)

Meaningful and memorable, but deeply upsetting – that was the import of this mournful extended play on words woven by Micah around the towns and villages of the Shephelah. These places would suffer grievously as the invading army came right up to the gate of Jerusalem (verse 9). Those who managed to escape would have to flee to the nearby hiding places of Adullam (verse 15), as David and his companions had done over 250 years before when Saul was trying to catch and kill them (1 Samuel 22:1-2). Their fate was sealed, and there was not much they could do other than shave their heads completely as a sign of mourning for their coming captivity (verse 16, see box, left).

Head shaving (Micah 1:16)

Certain Canaanite ways of shaving the hair were forbidden to the children of Israel because they were associated with idolatrous practices:

➤ *"You shall not shave around the sides of your head, nor shall you disfigure the edges of your beard"* (Leviticus 19:27).

➤ *"You are the children of the LORD your God: you shall not cut yourselves nor shave the front of your head for the dead"* (Deuteronomy 14:1).

But not all shaving of the head was forbidden under the Law of Moses. It was commanded in connection with the fulfilment of a Nazarite vow:

➤ *"When the days of his separation are fulfilled ... The Nazarite shall shave his consecrated head at the door of the tabernacle of meeting"* (Numbers 6:13,18).

➤ Samson was dedicated by his parents as a Nazarite from his birth (Judges 13:5), and the shaving of his head by Delilah and the Philistines was clearly linked to the loss of Samson's phenomenal strength (Judges 16:17-22).

➤ The Apostle Paul may have been under some form of Nazarite vow in Acts 18:18, when he *"had his hair cut off at Cenchrea".*

For Job, the shaving of the head seems to have been a natural response to his terrible sufferings (Job 1:20); and this was no doubt what it would signify for those in Judah who were to suffer such dreadful distress at the hands of the Assyrian invaders.

* *Peake's Commentary on the Bible* (Wokingham, Van Nostrand, 1986), page 631.

If, as suggested here, the prophecy about the destruction of Samaria (in verses 3-7) was first delivered by Micah towards the end of the 16-year reign of Jotham (758-742 BC), there can be little doubt that the prophet would continue to repeat these same ominous warnings to Israel as the time for the prophecy's fulfilment (721 BC) drew nearer.

Micah will also have repeated, perhaps many times over a period of years, the prophecy about the invasion of Judah (verses 8-16). While Judah may have thought it was safe after the Assyrians had defeated Israel and left (2 Kings 18:9-12), it was Micah's job to keep emphasising to Judah throughout the wicked reign of Ahaz (742-726 BC) that Jerusalem and the villages of the Shephelah would share the same fate as Samaria.

There were no doubt many occasions when verses 8-16, and the noisy lamentation of the prophet which accompanied them, were heard in the nation's capital and in the streets of Judah's towns and villages once they had been recaptured by Hezekiah from the domination of the Philistines (2 Kings 18:8 and 2 Chronicles 28:18,19). And when Sennacherib's last invasion of Judah finally brought about the grim fulfilment of Micah's worst fears for the inhabitants of the Shephelah in 701 BC, it was only thanks to Hezekiah's faithful prayer to God that the all-conquering Assyrians were turned back from Jerusalem, by Divine intervention, and the destruction of the city was deferred.

2:1-11 – "For this is an evil time"

Bearing in mind that there were no chapter divisions in the Hebrew text, it's perfectly possible to see Micah 2:1-11 as an integral part of the prophecies against Samaria and Judah in Micah 1. Seen in that light, these verses contain the detailed reasons for God's displeasure with His people, and for the punishments He had decided to bring on both the northern and the southern kingdoms. In summary – and this was especially (though not uniquely) true of the reign of Ahaz – the time in which Micah was prophesying was "an evil time" (2:3).

The time was evil because the laws of God were being broken in every conceivable way:

- **2:1** – There were people in Israel and Judah spending all their waking hours weaving wicked plots, even while they were in bed (like the archetypal wicked person described in Psalm 36:4, who *"devises wickedness on his bed"*). They must have forgotten that one of the six things that God hates was *"a heart that devises wicked plans"* (Proverbs 6:18). In fact, they were so brazen about it that they didn't even wait until the cover of darkness to put their evil schemes into effect. So Micah described the chilling process, from the evil thought to the wicked deed, as all these efforts to make money by illegal means were systematically *"devised ... worked out ... and practised"*. Evil was being done as if

for fun – people did it 'just because they could'.

- **2:2** – In direct contravention of the Law of Moses, fields and houses belonging to others were being stolen through oppression (just as in the days of Ahab, when Naboth's vineyard was violently seized – 1 Kings 21). The ownership of land was regarded as the very basis of a settled life in the Promised Land: it was a family possession to be handed down through the generations as a sacred trust.

- **2:6 (and 11)** – Most people had no interest in the word of God. *"Do not prattle"* (margin, literally, 'drip words') was apparently a common insult to God's prophets. Perhaps this gives us a small insight into the kind of opposition that Micah encountered as he went about preaching God's word. When Micah told them what would happen to them if they did not change their ways, their reaction was: 'We don't want to hear about such things – they will never happen to us'. They preferred to choose as their favourite 'prattler' the prophets that God had not sent – and especially those whose words 'dripped' with wine and strong drink (verse 11).

- **2:8,9** – It was a time of extortion, too, when nobody was free from personal danger – when men who thought they were as safe as soldiers returning from battle were being stripped of their best clothes; when defenceless women were being evicted from their family homes; and when even young children were being cruelly deprived of the good things which God had provided for them. (There is a foretaste here of the wickedness condemned by the Lord Jesus and practised by the scribes, who 'devoured' widows' houses in the first century – Mark 12:40.)

This sickening catalogue of wrongdoing – which didn't include the idolatry, immorality and deceit which Micah was to renounce in later prophecies – was one of the main reasons why Micah was sent to threaten God's people with punishment. And it's worth noting that embedded within these verses were God's personal responses to such human wickedness, couched in strong irony:

- **2:3-5** – Because the people had spent their time devising evil and robbing their neighbours of their property (2:1-2), God Himself was "devising disaster" against them (verse 3): He would ensure that their own inheritance was taken away, and that their fate would become proverbial. Their punishment would press heavily on them, like a yoke on the neck of an animal, as they saw their own fields taken violently, and as the prospect of any part in a future distribution of land by lot was removed from them and given to the invader (described in the NKJV as a *"turncoat"*, but in other versions as *"apostate"* or *"heathen"*).

- **2:6,7** – Micah's audience tried to stop him prophesying by seeking to humiliate him (*"Do not prattle"*, they said – verse 6). They prided themselves in being known as *"the house of Jacob"* (verse 7), and yet they were prepared to belittle God's true prophets (like Micah). They refused to accept that Micah really was speaking the words of God, so he and the other true prophets would no longer speak to them, nor would they *"return insult for insult"* (verse 6). The evildoers might not want to believe that their punishments, when they arrived, were God's doing; but the Spirit of God could not be restricted or denied, and the genuine prophets would go and speak God's words to anyone in Judah who could be described as walking *"uprightly"*. Such people would recognise God's word when it came to them, and it would do them good.

- **2:10** – Because these wicked people had evicted so many of their neighbours and fellow-countrymen from their property, God Himself would drive them out into captivity. They thought they had now finally entered into the 'rest' that God had promised them (Deuteronomy 12:9,10); but because they had defiled the Land of Promise, Canaan would cast them out, to their *"utter destruction"*.

If anyone took the trouble to listen to Micah, they would be left in no doubt about

what was coming, and they would certainly know the reasons why …

> **(B) 2:12-13: DELIVERANCE FOR A REMNANT**

2:12 – "Like a flock in the midst of their pasture"

It's a recurring feature of the prophetic word of God that, however dark the future may be painted, or however dire the predictions of punishment may seem, there is almost always a silver lining to every storm cloud. And Micah's prophecies were no exception.

From the beginning of this first section of Micah (in 1:2) until this point (2:11), the tone and content of the prophet's message had been characterised by unrelieved gloom. But now, however briefly, the veil of darkness and destruction was momentarily pulled away, and there was a glimpse of a more distant future, in which a regathered remnant* of God's people would one day live safely like sheep in their fold, or in the quietness of their pasture, with their eternal ruler as their shepherd.

It's not beyond the bounds of possibility that these few words of comfort were not even heard by the evildoers, since they preferred not to listen to the words of the Spirit of God speaking through Micah. Indeed, it seems more than likely that this

The effect of God's words

The effect of God's words on different people:

> *"Do not my words do good to him who walks uprightly?"*
> (Micah 2:7)

In Micah 2:7, God Himself is making a really important statement about the effect of His words on different people:

➤ **To the wicked**, God's words are unacceptable: they would simply prefer not to hear them.

➤ **To the 'upright'** (where the Hebrew word *yashar* means 'straight', or 'just'), God's words 'are pleasant' (the literal meaning of *"do good"*), and they are happy to receive them and act on them.

---

* The word *"remnant"* is always used in the prophets to mean the survivors of a Divine judgement (see, for example, Isaiah 10:20-22).

brilliant ray of hope was heard and understood only by the few 'upright' ones to whom Micah was obliged to turn to find a receptive audience. In that sense, therefore, these two lovely verses, with their message of ultimate salvation, would have appeared, in their contemporary setting, as examples of the words of God doing *"good"* (being 'pleasant') to *"him who walks uprightly"* (verse 7).

For us, over 2,700 years since these words of Micah were first spoken, this promise of a time of peace for the people of God under a Shepherd-King speaks in clear tones about the still future kingdom of Jesus Christ on earth. This is a consistent Bible theme which began as far back as Jacob's blessing on his son Judah (Genesis 49:8-12). The same promise surfaced again in the oracles of Balaam (Numbers 24). It found its most complete expression in Psalm 72; and it ran through the writings of the Old Testament prophets (such as, for example, Isaiah 11, Jeremiah 23, Ezekiel 36:33-8, Daniel 12:13, and Zechariah 13). This was the promised kingdom of God on earth of which Jesus himself preached the good news in the first century AD.

And this same message of hope for Israel's future (what the Apostle Paul called *"the hope of Israel"* in Acts 28:20) was spread across the New Testament world by the disciples of Jesus, including the Apostle Peter, who spoke about Jesus being in heaven *"until the times of restoration of all things, which God has spoken by the mouth of all His holy prophets* (including Micah, of course!) *since the world began"* (Acts 3:21).

Informed by all these 'words of God', revealed in other parts of the Bible, it becomes clear to us, 27 centuries after Micah's time, that Micah, in these two short verses, was contributing to the longer-term picture of the reign of Jesus Christ on earth, and was taking his place in the long sequence of prophets who looked forward to the culmination of God's purpose with the earth. Like many faithful men and

What is the Hope of Israel?

Here's an exercise in Bible study for you to try out for yourself.

'The Hope of Israel' (or 'Jacob's hope') is a Biblical expression used to summarise God's promises to the fathers of the Jewish nation (Abraham, Isaac and Jacob) about the whole purpose of God with the earth and His plans for the deliverance of men and women from sin and death through the work of His Son Jesus Christ.

See if you can find eight different aspects of 'the Hope of Israel' by looking up and reading all the Bible passages listed below. (Try to find one aspect in each passage if you can.)

➤ Genesis 49:10   ➤ Numbers 24:7   ➤ Psalm 72:8   ➤ Isaiah 11:9
➤ Jeremiah 23:5   ➤ Ezekiel 36:35   ➤ Daniel 12:13   ➤ Zechariah 14:8,9

There are many more aspects to 'the Hope of Israel' than this; but looking up these passages and analysing them carefully should give you a much clearer idea of what the Bible teaches on this important topic. [Outline answers are given on page 67.]

"For the hope of Israel I am bound with this chain" (Acts 28:20).

women before him, Micah looked forward to the day when, as the Apostle John described it so movingly, the people of God *"shall neither hunger any more nor thirst any more ... for the Lamb who is in the midst of the throne will shepherd them and lead them to living fountains of waters. And God will wipe away every tear from their eyes"* (Revelation 7:16,17).

And yet, for the faithful few in Micah's day, and no doubt also for the prophet himself, the 'silver lining' represented by this promise of future restoration and peace almost certainly contained a prospect of fulfilment much closer in time to the evil days of the eighth century BC. A wise and experienced writer on Bible matters once wrote that "the prophet's **primary** work was the work of his own living presence in Israel".* And this fits in well with the Divine principle expressed through the prophet Jeremiah, that *"the prophet who prophesies of peace, when the word of the prophet comes to pass, the prophet will be known as one whom the LORD has truly sent"* (Jeremiah 28:9).

So when we take all this into account and consider Micah a little more carefully in the context of his own time, the following points emerge to suggest that perhaps these verses in Micah 2 had a **primary** fulfilment in the lifetime of the prophet:

---

* Robert Roberts, *The Ministry of the Prophets*, page 4.

- Micah 2:12,13 comes immediately after the prophecies predicting the captivity of Samaria (1:3-7) and the capture of the towns and villages of the Judean Shephelah (1:8-16). In historical terms, the first was fulfilled in 721 BC, and the second (partially at least) in 719, 713 and 701 BC, during the various Assyrian campaigns against Philistia, Egypt and Judah. Micah's prophecies of doom were therefore shown to be accurate within only a matter of years of being pronounced. That being so, why should his prophecy of restoration and peace not also come to pass in some similarly contemporary way, especially in view of the Divine principle expressed by Jeremiah?

- While the northern kingdom of Israel was taken into captivity and the southern kingdom of Judah was initially devastated by the Assyrians, Jerusalem was not overrun until very much later. In fact, as 2 Kings 18-20 and 2 Chronicles 29-32 make clear, Sennacherib's army was turned back by Divine intervention, and Hezekiah presided over a short 'golden age' of peace around the end of the 8th century BC. This was a clear illustration of another important Divine principle: *"If that nation against whom I have spoken turns from its evil, I will relent of the disaster that I thought to bring upon it"* (Jeremiah 18:8);

- This time of peace under Hezekiah also gave a remnant of God's people a

Parallels between Hezekiah and Jesus

Both Hezekiah and Jesus:

➤ Cleansed the temple.

➤ Prayed for their people (and were heard).

➤ Offered sacrifices for themselves and for others.

➤ Provided 'living' water.

➤ Destroyed the adversary with God's help.

➤ Were miraculously cured of an 'incurable' disease.

➤ Brought the people of God out of captivity.

➤ Received gifts and homage.

➤ Were / will be acknowledged as King by the nations.

➤ Ruled / will rule over a golden age of peace and prosperity.

(With acknowledgements to Harry Whittaker)

"The one who breaks open" (Micah 2:13)

More often than not in scripture, it is God Himself Who does the 'breaking'. For example:

➤ 1 Chronicles 15:13 – *"... the LORD our God broke out against us"* [referring to the 'breach' which God made on Uzzah in 2 Samuel 6:8].

➤ Job 16:14 – *"He* [God] *breaks me with wound upon wound."*

➤ Psalm 2:9 – *"You shall break them with a rod of iron."*

➤ Psalm 107:16 – *"He* [God] *has broken the gates of bronze."*

➤ Isaiah 5:5 – *"I will ... break down its wall."*

➤ Isaiah 14:25 – *"I will break the Assyrian in my land."*

➤ Isaiah 45:2 – *"I will break in pieces the gates of bronze."*

When Sennacherib is described in 2 Chronicles 32:1 as coming up against Judah *"thinking to win ... over to himself"* the nation's *"fortified cities"*, the word translated *"to win over"* means 'to cleave, or to break' (as noted in the margin of the Authorised Version). Having taken to himself God's role as *"the one who breaks"*, it is therefore highly appropriate that it was Sennacherib who ended up being broken (Isaiah 14:25; 2 Kings 19:35-37).

According to E.B. Pusey *(The Minor Prophets ... Micah*, page 310), many ancient Jewish authorities recognised *"the one who breaks open"* as one of the titles of the Messiah, who "breaks the prison bars of the captives ... and leads them out at the gate of the city". Picking up the sheep / shepherd imagery, John Marsh *(Amos and Micah,* page 100) says that "the breaker is the ram who, by pushing with his strong horns, makes a way through ... for the flock".

There is every reason, therefore, to regard God Himself as *"the breaker"*, with His work carried out for Him, first by the angel of destruction who lifted the siege of Jerusalem by destroying Sennacherib's army, and secondly through the work of the Lord Jesus Christ when he saves God's people from destruction at his Second Coming.

"The breaker and the King are both metaphors for God" (John Marsh).

small foretaste of the greater deliverance which is still to come, with Hezekiah himself serving as a type of the Lord Jesus Christ in his role as Shepherd, Messiah and King. Language associated with sheep and shepherds occurs not only here in this Messianic passage, but also in each of Micah's other prophecies of ultimate deliverance (4:6-8; 5:4,5; and 7:14). The direct parallels between the lives of Hezekiah and Christ (as King over God's people) are so remarkable and so numerous, that an earlier writer was led to conclude that "those who study the life of Hezekiah with care will find themselves much better equipped to understand many of the Messianic features of Psalms and prophets".*

2:13 – The "one who breaks open"

The same parallelism occurs also in verse 13, where there is a word-play on the idea of 'breaking open' (the Hebrew *parats* means 'to make a breach'). Jerusalem was delivered from the besieging Assyrian army by the angel of the Lord, who 'broke out' of the besieged city to go into the invaders' camp, where he slew 185,000 of them in one night (2 Kings 19:35). According to 2 Chronicles 32:1, it had been Sennacherib's firm intention, in invading Judah, to *"win them (i.e. the fortified*

---

* Harry Whittaker, *Hezekiah the Great* (Birmingham, The Christadelphian, 1985), page v.

cities) over to himself". The Hebrew word translated "win over" (Hebrew baqa) means 'to break up' (see AV margin). Sennacherib, in other words, was thinking of himself as "the one who breaks", spoken of by Micah (2:13).

But as things turned out, it was the besieged citizens of Jerusalem who were able to 'break out', in fulfilment of Micah's prophecy, while Sennacherib was the one who was broken, returning in shame to Nineveh, where he was assassinated by two

of his own sons (2 Kings 19:36,37). Both at the time of Hezekiah, therefore, and at the coming of Christ to save the remnant of God's people, the saviour was to be the "one who breaks open" with Divine power. As another writer says, "... in the light of other prophecies, [this conqueror] can be no other than the Messiah."* The power to 'break' will remain in the hands of the Almighty, and "their king will pass before them, with the LORD at their head" (Micah 2:13).

Questions on Part one (outline answers on page 67)

1.1 Visions of God like the one described in Micah 1:2-4 are sometimes referred to as a 'theophany' (literally: God manifestation). What particular features does this theophany share in common with the vision described in Nahum 1:2-8 (which is a prophecy about God's judgements against Assyria)?

1.2 What does the fact that the people of Judah still went on sinning after they had seen God bring punishment on the people of northern Israel tell us about human nature?

1.3 In view of the fact that Micah made so many references to the Pentateuch, what occupation may he have had before he became a prophet?

1.4 Why was prostitution (1:7) used to represent the worship of other gods?

1.5 Why was it such a bad thing to take another person's land (2:2)?

1.6 In his Sermon on the Mount, the Lord Jesus warned that "with the measure you use, it will be measured back to you" (Matthew 7:2). With that in mind, what were the very appropriate punishments that Micah said would come for a) working out evil (2:1); b) violently robbing people of their fields (2:2); and c) seizing other people's houses (2:2)?

* T. K. Cheyne, *Micah, with notes and introduction* (Cambridge University Press, 1891), page 29.

Part two (3:1 to 5:15)

"HEAR NOW, O HEADS OF JACOB"

(A) 3:1-12: JUDGEMENT ON JUDAH'S LEADERS

A natural break between the end of chapter 2 and the opening of a new section of Micah's prophecies is created by the tell-tale phrase *"And I said"* at the beginning of chapter 3. This provides a hint that the seven chapters of Micah that have come down to us consist of Micah's inspired selection of edited highlights from the many prophecies he had spoken over the years. Micah's editorial work on his own prophecies is also indicated by the fairly obvious three-fold division of the prophecy: all three parts begin with a call to *"Hear"*, which acts as a structural indicator (1:2; 3:1 and 6:1), and each part contains Divine judgements followed by the promise of deliverance and restoration.*

Addressed to the *"heads of Jacob"* and the *"rulers of the house of Israel"* (verse 1), the twelve verses of condemnation that

---

* This is the basis of the three-part structure of Micah summarised on page 13.

---

followed fall naturally into three subsets of four verses each, and this may be further evidence of Micah's editorial activity. The first subset (verses 1-4) targeted the leaders of the nation; the second (verses 5-8) was aimed at the false prophets; and the third (verses 9-12) put them all in the dock together.

3:1-4 – No justice from the rulers

Micah accused the rulers not so much of **lacking in judgement** as of **failing to exercise justice**. (Justice is an important concept in Micah, and the New King James Version accurately captures this at the end of verse 1 by translating the Hebrew *mishpat* as "justice".) The rulers had responsibilities as the magistrates of God's people; but they were falling down in their duty of dispensing the proper code of justice which had been laid down in the Law of Moses. Micah went so far as to suggest that the rulers had never even taken the trouble to learn the laws of God: they did not *"know justice"* (verse 1). They hated good and loved evil (verse 2); and they oppressed the people to such an extent, by perverting justice to their own financial advantage, that Micah was justified in describing them as butchers. They spent their time slaughtering, cooking and eating the defenceless flock which they ought to have been protecting (verses 2,3). Their punishment would come in the day when they turned to God for help only to find Him with His face hidden from them, his ears deaf to their pleas, leaving them to the fate that they deserved (verse 4). In effect, because they had failed to learn and practise the justice of God, they would have to learn

The Lord 'hides His face' (Micah 3:4)

The source passage for this expression is Deuteronomy 31:17,18, where God told Moses in no uncertain terms what would happen if His people Israel were ever unfaithful to the covenant they had made with Him:

> *"My anger shall be aroused against them in that day, and I will forsake them, and I will **hide my face from them**, and they shall be devoured. And many evils and troubles shall befall them, so that they will say in that day, 'Have not these evils come upon us because our God is not among us?' And I will surely **hide my face** in that day because of all the evil which they have done, in that they have turned to other gods."*

That day had now come, and it was Micah's task to remind God's people that the hiding of God's face from them would bring serious trouble in its wake. It was the opposite of God's face 'shining upon' them (Numbers 6:25). Other occurrences of the same phrase show how devastating it can be when God looks away and the favour of His presence is removed:

➤ Job 13:24 – *"Why do you hide your face, and **regard me as your enemy?"***

➤ Psalm 69:17 – *"Do not hide your face from your servant, for **I am in trouble**."*

➤ Psalm 143:7 – *"Do not hide your face from me, **lest I be like those who go down into the pit**."*

➤ Isaiah 8:17 – *"And I will wait on the LORD, who hides his face from the house of Jacob."* (Isaiah used the same language as Micah – another sign that he and Micah were contemporaries – see Appendix.)

➤ Isaiah 64:7 – *"There is no one who calls on your name, who stirs himself up to take hold of you; for you have hidden your face from us, and have **consumed us because of our iniquities**."*

➤ Ezekiel 39:23,24 – *"... the house of Israel went into captivity for their iniquity; because they were unfaithful to me, therefore I hid my face from them. I gave them **into the hand of their enemies, and they all fell by the sword**. According to their uncleanness and according to their transgressions I have dealt with them, and hidden my face from them."*

But God also made a solemn promise that there would one day come a time when he would no longer hide His face from Israel: *"I will not hide my face from them any more; for I shall have poured out my Spirit on the house of Israel, says the Lord GOD"* (Ezekiel 39:29).

it the hard way, by having it visited on them.

3:5-8 – Misdeeds of the false prophets

The false prophets were the next targets of Micah's fierce criticism. Like the magistrates who were supposed to dispense proper justice, the prophets were abusing their privileged position. They should have spoken the words of God; but instead they were making God's people *"stray"* (the original word in verse 5 means 'to wander out of the way'); they gave false comfort, by speaking of peace when war was coming; and like snakes, they bit and

declared 'holy war' on anybody who refused to feed them (i.e. pay their bribes!).

Their punishment for all these misdeeds would be to have the prophetic gift withdrawn from them altogether: it would 'go dark' on them (verse 6), and they would receive no more visions or revelations from God. Figuratively speaking, *"the sun"* (of God's prophetic insight) would go down on them, and they would be ashamed because they never had any genuine messages (verse 7). Like lepers (see Leviticus 13:45) they would have to *"cover their lips"*, because there was *"no answer from God"*.

By complete contrast, Micah was able to claim Divine authority and power for his own prophetic calling and ministry: he spoke *"by the Spirit of the LORD"*, and his words were full of Divine justice, powerfully convicting *"Jacob"* and *"Israel"* of their sinfulness (verse 8).

3:9-12 – A false sense of security

Micah aimed his criticism once again at the false prophets and the rulers, and also added a word or two against the priests for good measure (verse 11). He repeated his accusation against the leaders for hating and perverting justice (verse 9), and he railed against the crimes they were committing within God's holy city (verse 10). But money talked, even louder than Micah: the judges took bribes; the priests sought fees for their work; and the false prophets were no better than well-paid fortune-tellers (verse 11). Yet they claimed (falsely) to *"lean on the LORD"* (the word

Micah 3:5 – chewing or biting?

"... they chew with their teeth" (Micah 3:5, New King James Version) is not a particularly good translation of the Hebrew word *nashak*. Wherever else it occurs, the word is almost always translated *"bite"*, and is primarily associated with snakes, as in the following examples from other passages in the Old Testament:

► Numbers 21:6 – *"So the Lord sent fiery serpents among the people, and they bit the people; and many of the people of Israel died."*

► Proverbs 23:31-32 – *"Do not look on the wine when it is red ... At the last it bites like a serpent and stings like a viper."*

► Amos 9:3 – *"Though they hide from my sight at the bottom of the sea, from there I will command the serpent, and it shall bite them."*

Micah's condemnation of the false prophets of his time becomes much more vivid, therefore, when we realise that, like Jesus in later years (Matthew 3:7), Micah was describing them as serpents: they were liars, like the serpent in Eden, and their lies caused others to sin.

"lean" is the same as *"relied"* in 2 Chronicles 13:18, *"rest on"* in 2 Chronicles 14:11, and *"depend on"* in Isaiah 10:20). Their sense of security may have been based on the well-known sign that God had given to King Ahaz through Isaiah some years before. Ahaz was promised that his virgin bride would have a son and that the child's name would be Immanuel, meaning 'God is with us' (Isaiah 7:14). The birth of this child (Hezekiah) shortly after the wicked reign of Ahaz began,* may well have been taken by the population of Jerusalem generally as a sign that their city was safe; and this could be reflected in their complacent comment: *"Is not the LORD among us? No harm can come upon us"* (verse 11).

What a shock it must have been for these rulers to hear Micah brutally undermine their misplaced confidence! Divine security could only be enjoyed on the basis of moral obedience and sincere worship. But their ungodly world of social injustice was going to be brought to a sudden end. Because of their wickedness, God's holy hill of Zion would be ploughed flat like an open field, the proud and ancient city of Jerusalem would be turned into *"heaps of ruins"*, and the temple mount itself would be laid as bare as hills above the tree-line (verse 12).

Rarely, if ever, has the destruction of Jerusalem been predicted in such

* See Harry Whittaker, *Isaiah* (Cannock, Biblia, 1988), page 149.

uncompromising terms. Small wonder, then, that these threatening words of Micah were to move Hezekiah to fear God and to seek His forgiveness on behalf of the nation. It was thanks to Hezekiah's timely reformation that the predicted destruction of the nation's capital was averted, for the time being at least (2 Kings 18). Nor is it at all surprising that the effect of this powerful prophecy from Micah was still remembered over a century later in the time of King Jehoiakim, when the memory of it was instrumental in saving the life of the prophet Jeremiah (Jeremiah 26:12-24).

Micah's prophecy about the destruction of Jerusalem was eventually fulfilled by the Babylonians, in about 586 BC. But it's also possible to see even later fulfilments of the prophecy: in the fall of Jerusalem to the Romans in AD 70, and especially in the ploughing of the site of Jerusalem by Hadrian in AD 135, as foretold also by the Lord Jesus himself in terms not unlike those of Micah (see Luke 19:44).

> **(B) 4:1-5:15: DELIVERANCE FOR ZION AND VENGEANCE ON THE NATIONS**

In a dramatic change of tone which is a common feature of each of the three major divisions of Micah's prophecy, the grim threat of overthrow and destruction at the end of chapter 3 is once again immediately followed by the prospect of a wonderful

"Zion shall be ploughed like a field" (Micah 3:12)

'Judea capta': Judea captive

Coin of the Emperor Vespasian celebrating victory over the First Jewish Revolt, AD 70

'Aelia Capitolina': Hadrian's capital

Coin of the Emperor Hadrian depicting the ploughing of the site of Jerusalem, AD 135

"Richardson, visiting Jerusalem in the middle of the nineteenth century, records concerning the sacred ground of Zion: 'One part of it supported a crop of barley, another was undergoing the labour of the plough.'"   (R.F. Horton)

restoration. In this case, however, the good news is two whole chapters long, by contrast with the two short verses of deliverance in chapter 2 (verses 12,13).

The division between chapters 4 and 5 – though not part of the original Hebrew text – serves as a useful marker, with the emphasis in chapter 4 being on **Zion's coming deliverance and triumph**, and with chapter 5 depicting **the promise of the coming Saviour and the destruction of the enemies of 'Jacob'**, beginning with the defeat of the Assyrians in verses 5,6.

4:1-5 – The Lord's reign in Zion

Chapter 4 begins with five breathtaking verses which deliberately counterbalance the closing verses of the previous chapter. In 3:9-12, Jerusalem was going to be laid waste; but in 4:1-5, the holy city would be *"exalted"*: it would become a centre of spiritual education and justice for other nations (verses 1-3); it would enjoy a time of peace and prosperity (verses 3,4); and those who were once in the habit of worshipping their own gods would pledge themselves to serve the God of Israel for ever (verse 5).

Micah 4:1-5 is a famous passage which contains many important expressions and ideas; and these five verses must have stood out like a beacon among Micah's many prophetic pronouncements – and especially for the faithful (the 'upright' of 2:7). The idea that *"peoples"* would *"flow"* to Jerusalem, and that *"many nations"* would want to go up to the city to learn the ways

of the God of Jacob (4:1,2), must have been a very exciting prospect for Micah himself – and not least because in his day he had received such a poor hearing from most of the inhabitants of Jerusalem. Micah must also have been pleased to think that, one day, 'all roads would lead to Jerusalem', thus reversing the effects of the Tower of Babel (Genesis 11), and drawing the nations of the earth back to God to learn of Him in peace.

The notion that one day God's law, and His word, would issue from Jerusalem, bringing judgement (justice) to *"many peoples"* (verses 2,3) must have gladdened the hearts of any faithful ones who heard Micah speak, as well as of those who have read and believed these words long after Micah passed off the scene. The hope that the Lord, in the future time known as *"the latter days"*, would oblige even the *"strong nations"* (verse 3) to turn their weapons of destruction into peaceful instruments of agriculture, and that no nation would never again become expert in war, has been an objective that has eluded mankind almost since the dawn of history. What a great irony it is that the United Nations, which has been struggling (and largely failing) since its establishment in 1945 to preserve world peace, should have a massive Russian statue outside its New York headquarters the title of which is a quotation of these very words from Micah 4:3.

And not only the United Nations in modern times, but also – much closer in time to Micah himself – the prophet Isaiah

"In the latter days" (Micah 4:1)

At the time when Micah used this surprisingly uncommon expression, which occurs only 12 times in the whole of the Old Testament, it had been used only three (or possibly four) times before:

➤ The prophet Balaam used it when he told Balak, king of Moab: "*I will advise you what this people* (i.e. Israel) *will do to your people* (Moab) *in the latter days …*" (Numbers 24:14);

➤ Moses used it twice in his final series of addresses to the children of Israel, in connection with a time of trouble for Israel from which God would ultimately deliver them:

  – First, he said: "*… you will seek the Lord your God, and you will find him … when you are in distress, and all these things come upon you in the latter days, when you turn to God and obey his voice*" (Deuteronomy 4:29,30);

  – Secondly, in his 'Song', Moses said: "*… evil will befall you in the latter days, because you will do evil in the sight of the Lord, to provoke him to anger through the work of your hands*" (Deuteronomy 31:29);

➤ The prophet Hosea used it in a prophecy addressed to the northern ten-tribe kingdom of Israel, which probably dates from slightly earlier than Micah's prophecies (though the two prophets did overlap to some extent). Hosea wrote: "*The children of Israel shall return and seek the Lord their God and David their king. They shall fear the Lord and his goodness in the latter days*" (Hosea 3:5).

In using this expression, therefore, Micah would be looking forward to a time when the children of Israel would have dominion over the children of Moab, when they would turn to God in distress and obey Him, when 'David their king' would rule over them again, and when they would once more find and enjoy the goodness of God through their repentance. All of these elements, combined with Micah's vision of a time when Jerusalem would become the religious capital of the world in an era of universal peace, **suggest that the prophet was looking to what was then a distant future**.

This view – that the phrase "*the latter days*" has to do with a time towards the very end of man's history – is confirmed by two other relevant facts:

1 The Hebrew expression itself (meaning literally 'at the end of the days') signifies "the line which formed the prophet's horizon" (R.F. Horton);

2 All of the remaining occurrences of the phrase in the Old Testament are consistent with the picture that Micah paints of the children of Israel turning finally to God in repentance at a time of trouble out of which Jerusalem emerges supreme, with Israel's Messiah ruling over the earth (Jeremiah 23:20; 30:24; 48:47; 49:39; Ezekiel 38:16; Daniel 2:28; 10:14).

In the light of all this, there appears to be good justification for thinking that "*the latter days*" is a prophetic phrase designating the time-period between the first and the second comings of Jesus, and therefore including our own twenty-first century.

"They shall beat their swords into plowshares"

This impressive statue by the Russian sculptor Yevgeny Vuchetich stands in the gardens of the United Nations building in New York. It is ironic that the statue was presented to the UN by the former Soviet Union during the Cold War, when Russia was at its most threatening and warlike! Beneath the sinewy man of bronze is a plaque quoting Micah's words of optimism about a future time of universal freedom from war.

quoted these very same words, using Micah's message of hope as the basis for his own preaching (compare Isaiah 2:2-4 and Micah 4:1-3, which are virtually identical). (Bible students have often differed about whether Micah quoted Isaiah or Isaiah quoted Micah; but one authoritative commentator has written: "It is now owned, well nigh on all hands, that the great prophecy [i.e. Micah 4:1-5], three verses of which Isaiah prefixed to his second chapter, was originally delivered by Micah … No one now thinks that Micah adopted that great prophecy from Isaiah".[1] We do well therefore to remember that in classifying Micah as one of 'The Minor Prophets', we are referring only to the length of his surviving writings and not to the strength of his impact upon his contemporaries.[2]

In fact, these verses were so well known in the time of Hezekiah that even the chief steward of Sennacherib's household was able to make an ironic reference to Micah's promise about the time when everyone would be able to sit in safety *"under his vine and under his fig tree"* – an expression which was perhaps particularly appropriate coming from the lips of Micah the country-dweller (4:4), and which looked back fondly to the days of prosperity and safety under

Solomon's peaceful rule (1 Kings 4:25). *"Do not listen to Hezekiah"*, Rabshakeh called out to the people of Jerusalem, *"for thus says the king of Assyria: 'Make peace with me by a present and come out to me; and every one of you eat from his own vine and every one from his own fig tree' …"* (Isaiah 36:16).

So good was Rabshakeh's Hebrew, and such was his inside knowledge of the Jews' situation in Jerusalem, that one writer has suggested that he was perhaps "a renegade Jew who … had been the leader of the pro-Assyrian party in Jerusalem".[3] That would also help to explain how an Assyrian came to know the very words of one of Micah's prophecies. It is also possible that Rabshakeh's scornful mocking of Hezekiah's confidence in his God – *"Has any one of the gods of the nations delivered its land from the hand of the king of Assyria?"* (Isaiah 36:18) – was a deliberate reference to Micah's promise that Israel's God would enable His people to say: *"we will walk in the name of the LORD our God for ever"* (4:5). But what Rabshakeh and his heathen master Sennacherib had overlooked was the fact that *"the mouth of the LORD of hosts"* – the military name of God – had spoken this promise (4:4)!

1 – E. B. Pusey, *The Minor Prophets* (Oxford, Parker, 1860), page 289.

2 – See also: Reg Carr, "The Not-so-Minor Prophets", *The Testimony*, Volume 44 (1974), pages 214-217.

3 – Harry Whittaker, *Hezekiah the Great*, op.cit., pages 54,55.

Quotations made from the prophecy of Micah

Micah	Quoted by	Subject of quotation
3:10	Habakkuk (2:12)	Building up a city by bloodshed and iniquity
3:12	*"Certain of the elders of the land"* in the time of Jehoiakim, king of Judah (Jeremiah 26:17-19)	Prophecy about the destruction of Jerusalem
4:1-3	Isaiah (Isaiah 2:2-4)	Prophecy about Jerusalem as the religious centre of the world
4:3	The United Nations	*"Swords into plowshares"*
4:4	Rabshakeh (Isaiah 36:16)	Promise of dwelling safely, *"everyone … under his vine and under his fig tree"*
4:4	Zechariah (3:10)	*"Under his vine and under his fig tree"*
4:4	The Lord Jesus Christ, in calling Nathanael to follow him to the kingdom (John 1:48)	*"… under the fig tree"*
4:6	Zephaniah (3:19)	Promise that God will save *"the lame"* among the flock
5:2	The chief priests and scribes in the time of Herod the Great (Matthew 2:4-8)	Prophecy about the birth of a future shepherd-king in Bethlehem
5:2	People in the crowd arguing about where the Messiah would come from (John 7:42)	The Christ was to be born in Bethlehem (like David)
6:8	US President Jimmy Carter in his inaugural address, January 1977	The humility, mercy and justice that God requires
7:6	The Lord Jesus Christ (Matthew 10:35-36)	Division / antagonism between friends & within families
Multiple Messianic passages	The Lord Jesus Christ to the disciples on the road to Emmaus (Luke 24:27)	*"He expounded to them in all the scriptures the things concerning himself"*

Sheep and shepherd imagery in Micah

'Shepherd' was widely used in the ancient Near East as a title for a king.

It is very appropriate that a country prophet like Micah should use so many word-pictures related to the keeping of sheep. Much of Micah's pastoral language is Messianic in its ultimate fulfilment, while the imagery undoubtedly looks back to David, Israel's first Shepherd-King. 'The good shepherd' of John 10 is not very far away.

Micah	Sheep / shepherd imagery
2:12,13	*"I will surely assemble all of you, O Jacob. I will surely gather the remnant of Israel; I will put them together like sheep of the fold, like a flock in the midst of their pasture; they shall make a loud noise because of so many men. The one who breaks open* [the leading ram?] *will come up before them; they will break out, pass through the gate, and go out by it; their king will pass before them, with the* LORD *at their head."*
4:6-8	*"'In that day', says the* LORD*, I will assemble the lame, I will gather the outcast and those whom I have afflicted; I will make the lame a remnant, and the outcast a strong nation … And you, O tower of the flock, the stronghold of the daughter of Zion, to you it shall come, even the former dominion shall come."*
5:4-6	*"And he shall stand and feed his flock in the strength of the* LORD*, in the majesty of the name of the* LORD *his God; and they shall abide … And this one shall be peace. When the Assyrian comes into our land … we will raise against him seven shepherds and eight princely men. They shall waste* (Hebrew raah = 'shepherd' or 'feed') *with the sword the land of Assyria."*
5:8	*"And the remnant of Jacob shall be … like a young lion among flocks of sheep."*
7:14	*"Shepherd your people with your staff, the flock of your heritage, who dwell solitarily in a woodland, in the midst of Carmel; let them feed in Bashan and Gilead, as in days of old."*

"And when the Chief Shepherd appears, you will receive the crown of glory that does not fade away" (1 Peter 5:4).

4:6-8 – Zion's time of triumph

After the striking passage about Zion's deliverance from her enemies, Micah 4:6-8 fills out the picture of Zion's time of triumph. *"In that day"* at the beginning of verse 6 refers to *"the latter days"* of verse 1, and the description of the future golden age continues, with God's people being spoken of largely as 'the sheep of His flock':

- *"the lame"* would be brought together, even though there would be fewer of them after they had suffered the Divine judgements (verses 6,7). (The Hebrew word for *"lame"* here – *tsala* – is quite rare in scripture. It occurs only in Zephaniah 3:19 – where there is probably yet another quotation from Micah – and in Genesis 32:31, where it refers to Jacob's permanent disability after he had wrestled with the angel. There was a further possible back-reference to Jacob by Micah in the expression *"tower of the flock"* in verse 8 – see comments below).

- Even though they had been outcasts, God would make them a strong people once more, and He would reign over them in Zion for ever (verse 7).

- The *"former dominion"* (the royal self-government that God's people had previously enjoyed under their kings – especially David and Solomon) would be restored; and it would return to what Micah calls both *"the tower of the flock"* (Hebrew: *migdal eder*) and *"the stronghold* (Hebrew: *ophel*) of

the daughter of Zion" (verse 8) – two expressions that seem to bring together a location beyond Bethlehem where Jacob *"pitched his tent"* after the death of Rachel (Genesis 35:21), and the hill within the ancient city of Jerusalem (Ophel) which David took from the Jebusites and which both Jotham and Manasseh fortified (2 Samuel 5:7-9; 2 Chronicles 27:3 and 33:14). In view of what followed in Micah's next prophecy, in chapter 5, about Bethlehem being the future birthplace of the Messiah, these references to Jacob and David seem particularly appropriate, associated as both these characters were with God's eternal purpose with His people Israel.

4:9-13 – Zion's daughter: saved out of Babylon

It was, however, necessary for Micah to stress that Zion's ultimate triumph would come only after much suffering. In common with other prophets (like Isaiah, Jeremiah and Zephaniah), one of Micah's favourite phrases was *"the daughter of Zion"* (as in 1:13, 4:8 [twice], 4:10, and 4:13); and he used it to depict the city of Jerusalem as a woman crying out in labour pain (verse 9). The Hebrew word for 'city' is feminine, and *"she"* (Jerusalem) appears to have no king to prevent her – even while she was actually in labour – from being taken away into captivity in Babylon, where her child would eventually be born, and from where the Lord Himself would finally redeem her

(verse 10). The Hebrew for 'redeem' is *gaal* (literally: 'to act as the near kinsman', the one who had the right of redemption, as in Ruth 4:1-6); so God Himself would recover His people as a lost possession and restore them to their original status.

The mention of Babylon – the first and only time that it was named by Micah (whose prophecies are mostly set against the ascendancy of Assyria) – reminds us that the Babylonians were already beginning to make their presence felt on the international stage during Micah's lifetime. Isaiah, for example, recorded the occasion when a delegation of Babylonian envoys came to Jerusalem. They came, on the surface at least, to congratulate Hezekiah on his recovery from his serious illness, so it must have been around the year 713 BC. It was after Hezekiah had unwisely shown the delegation all the treasures he had amassed and they had gone back to Babylon, no doubt to report what they had seen to their lord Merodach-Baladan, that Hezekiah was told by Isaiah: *"Behold, the days are coming when all that is in your house … shall be carried to Babylon; nothing shall be left"* (Isaiah 39:6). So Micah was by no means the only prophet at that time to predict Judah's future captivity at the hands of the Babylonians.

It took more than a century for these predictions about the fall of Jerusalem to the Babylonians to be fulfilled; but Micah was quite categorical about the certainty of it: *"… you shall go even to Babylon"* (4:10). During the course of Judah's violation, too, many of Judah's enemies in the surrounding nations (Edom, Moab and Ammon, for example) would gloat over the city's distress and be pleased to see her nakedness (verse 11).

But whatever these enemies thought about Israel's God, He would not forget their behaviour, and the time would ultimately come for Him to gather them *"like sheaves to the threshing-floor"* (verse 12), where Zion would take her revenge on them. The labour pains would prove to be the painful beginnings of a process which would lead to salvation through suffering. They were to be, in effect, the birth-pangs of a new age. And so the chapter concludes with a picture of the once-humbled but now-restored *"daughter of Zion"* being given the Divine permission to *"thresh"* those nations like an ox with iron horns and bronze hooves (by which, presumably, the grain would be ground to a very fine powder).

"Many peoples" would be 'beaten in pieces' in the process; but their *"gain"* (the original word signifies 'wealth acquired by dishonest means') and their *"substance"* (the original word means 'forces', and is usually translated as 'army') would serve not so much to enrich and strengthen Judah: instead it would be dedicated to *"the Lord of the whole earth"* (verse 13). One of the titles which Sennacherib 'awarded' to himself in his pride was "King over the world", and this may well be an ironic reminder to Micah's contemporaries (and to us) that no man ought ever to be so foolish as to try to take that honour from God.

5:1-6 – The ruler in Israel: Hezekiah and Christ

Micah 5 is based firmly in the eighth century context of the siege of Jerusalem by the Assyrians and the destruction of Sennacherib's army. In its first fulfilment, this fifteen-verse prophecy was about King Hezekiah. In the Hebrew text, 5:1 stands as the final verse of the previous prophecy, and it operates as a kind of bridge between the two. The *"woman in labour"* (a symbol of Jerusalem in difficulties) in 4:9 appears again in 5:3, where she gives birth to a saviour who helps his people out of their troubles. The next five verses (2-6) foretell the coming of this great Messiah-King, who would come from Bethlehem (verse 2) to feed his people like a shepherd (verse 4) and to bring lasting peace after the Assyrian invasion of the land (verse 5). The rest of the chapter (verses 7-15) depicts the changes that would need to be made by God's new ruler: the vanquished remnant of God's people (verses 7-9) would be saved from their enemies and returned to the land; and God Himself would see to it that His people were cleansed from their waywardness as He re-established them safely (verses 10-15).

Micah 5:1-6 is another striking passage, full of language suggestive not only of Hezekiah, but also of Hezekiah's even more illustrious descendant, Jesus Christ. Micah prophesied first (verse 1) about a time when the *"daughter of troops"* (the city of Zion, 4:8) would be under siege. This would be a time when the city, so steeped in violence, would be subjected to violence by an external oppressor. It would also be a time when the nation's *"judge"* (the Hebrew word means *"ruler"*, as in the NIV) would be treated disgracefully. Hezekiah's personal humiliation by the insults of the sharp-tongued Assyrian envoy Rabshakeh (recounted in detail in Isaiah 36) was just a dim foretaste of the physical beating handed out to the Lord Jesus by the Romans (Matthew 27:27-31); yet it was clearly part of the parallel that Micah was drawing between Hezekiah and the true Messiah who would come so much later.

This opening verse (verse 1) is a really key one. Another writer describes it as "one more example of the way in which a prophecy, originally given in a particular situation and having significance for those who heard it, is found to have a wider and more prolonged sense than could at first have been expected, even extending to the final onslaught of the nations upon Jerusalem".* Verse 2 begins with the tiny word *"but"* – small in size, yet massive in meaning – and the scene is immediately changed from the lofty city of Jerusalem to the *"little town of Bethlehem"*.

Micah's contemporaries would know about Bethlehem as the humble birthplace of King David; and it's perfectly possible, as has been suggested by one Bible student,

---

* Fred Pearce, *From Hosea to Zephaniah,* op.cit., page 141.

that Hezekiah's mother may have gone there to wait for the birth of her royal son.[1] But for later readers like ourselves, this verse is about Jesus Christ, who was born, not in a royal palace, but in a stable in this otherwise insignificant village, described here as *"little among the thousands (or administrative units) of Judah"* (verse 2).

Yet in spite of its obscurity, Bethlehem, in the fruitful district of Ephrathah,[2] would be the place from where God's appointed ruler was to come to save God's people (verse 2). And the origins of that ruler would be intimately associated with the eternal God Himself: his *"goings forth are from of old, from everlasting"*. It's a great irony that the Jews themselves, from the time of Micah to the birth of Jesus, rightly regarded these verses as a prophecy about their Messiah; and yet ever since the birth of Jesus, the Jewish rabbis have struggled in vain to find a more obvious interpretation.[3]

But until the saviour came, *"the remnant of his brethren"* (most probably the survivors of the captives taken by Sennacherib during his Judean campaign)[4] would be 'given up' (i.e. 'remain') in captivity (verse 3). Only when the woman who was *"in labour"* had given birth would that captive remnant be joined again to the rest of the nation. And here, once again, we find a dual-fulfilment prophecy, in which both Hezekiah and the Lord Jesus can be seen as saviours who would *"stand and feed"* their *"flock"* like shepherds (verse 4), *"in the strength of the Lord his God"*, and be *"great to the ends of the earth"*. Both

of them would come to personify *"peace"* (verse 5) – Hezekiah *"when the Assyrian comes into our land, and when he treads in our palaces"*, and the Lord Jesus when he comes, as foreseen by Jacob in Genesis 49:10 as *"Shiloh"* (meaning 'peace') to save Israel from their latter-day invaders (depicted in Ezekiel 38 and Zechariah 12-14).[5]

The Messianic elements in this passage are inescapable; but it's clear, all the same, from the way that Micah played on the meaning of Hezekiah's name ("Whom Yah strengthens") in the phrase *"stand ... in the strength of the Lord"* (verse 4), that Micah was speaking **first**, and in his contemporary historical context, about the victory that Hezekiah would gain over the Assyrians and the reign of peace that would follow (2 Kings 20:19). As for the *"seven shepherds and* (NIV, "even") *eight princely men"* foreseen by Micah, who were to help God's mighty shepherd-ruler in his work against the enemies of God's people (verse 5), they may well have been particular royal counsellors who served Hezekiah; but there is no historical record of them, or of their work – prophesied here by Micah (verse 6) – in wasting (or 'feeding on') *"the land of Nimrod at its entrances"* (Assyria was part of Nimrod's kingdom – Genesis 10:11).

It's possible that the *"seven shepherds"* raised up against Assyria were the *"seven spirits"* of God (perhaps the archangels, Revelation 3:1), with Hezekiah himself making up the eight.[6] Others suggest that the numbers may be symbolic – seven of

1 – Harry Whittaker, *Hezekiah the Great,* op.cit., page 5.

2 – The Hebrew word *ephrathah* means 'fruitful'.

3 – "This great Messianic prophecy was always reckoned Messianic by the Jews until Christ was born in Bethlehem, when the difficult task of explaining it away had to begin." (R.F. Horton, *The Minor Prophets: Micah. The Century Bible, a Modern Commentary:* London, The Caxton Publishing Company, c. 1910, page 250)

4 – See Harry Whittaker, *Isaiah,* op.cit., page 27.

5 – Some commentators think *"the Assyrian"* (verse 5) was a cryptic name for all future enemies of Israel.

6 – Suggested by Harry Whittaker in *Hezekiah the Great,* op.cit., page 204.

Parallels between Hezekiah and the Lord Jesus in Micah 5

Micah 5	Hezekiah	Jesus
"They will strike the judge of Israel with a rod" (verse 1)	Humiliated by Rabshakeh	Hit with *"rods"* (See Matthew 26:67, AV margin)
"... out of you (Bethlehem Ephrathah) *shall come forth to me the one to be Ruler in Israel"* (verse 2)	Born in Bethlehem (?), perhaps as part of the sign to Ahaz	Born in Bethlehem
"... this one shall be peace" (verse 5)	Ruled in peace for part of his reign	Shiloh / *"The Prince of Peace"*
"When the Assyrian comes into our land ... we will raise against him seven shepherds and eight princely men" (verse 5)	Hezekiah and the seven archangels of God together successfully resisted Sennacherib (a suggestion of the late Harry Whittaker)	Reasonable to suppose that Jesus will have the assistance of these same angels in his victory over the nations
"They shall waste with the sword the land of Assyria ... at its entrances" (verse 6)	God's angels in control of the events leading to the death of Sennacherib and the sudden demise of Assyria	Jesus and the angels will destroy the enemies of the people of God
"... the remnant of Jacob shall be ... like dew from the LORD" (verse 7)	Hezekiah brought back the captive exiles	Jesus will raise the faithful from the sleep of death to a new life
"Like showers on the grass ..." (verse 7)	Renewal and reformation under Hezekiah	*"He shall come down like rain upon the mown grass"* (Psalm 72:6)
"Like a lion among the beasts of the forest" (verse 8)	*"... exalted in the sight of all nations"* (2 Chronicles 32:23)	*"The Lion of the tribe of Judah"* (Revelation 5:5)
"... all your enemies shall be cut off" (verse 9)	*"... the Lord saved Hezekiah from the hand of ... Assyria, and from the hand of all others"* (2 Chronicles 32:22)	*"Sit at my right hand, till I make your enemies your footstool"* (Psalm 110:1)
Judah to be purged of all that offends (verses 10-15)	Hezekiah's reformation cleansed the land	*"His winnowing fan is in his hand, and he will thoroughly clean out his threshing floor"* (Matthew 3:12)

completeness, and eight of sufficiency – as if to indicate that God would raise up **more than enough** for the task.*

5:7-9 – The roles of the rescued remnant

Micah depicted the rescued *"remnant"* of Judah with two quite distinct roles to play – both in the days of Hezekiah and, more completely when the Lord Jesus rules over God's people. First (in verse 7), the remnant was portrayed as acting like *"dew from the* LORD*"* upon the thirsty nations around. As Micah and his contemporaries were well aware from their own experience in Judah, during the hot and dry months of the year, plant life depended on the early morning dew for moisture and refreshment. Dew was therefore the ideal image by which to represent the spiritual blessings which would accompany Divine teaching. It spoke of a time when the nations would be taught God's saving Truth, as Moses taught the children of Israel in Deuteronomy 32:2 (*"Let my teaching drop as the rain, my speech distill as the dew"*). That time was perhaps briefly foreshadowed in Hezekiah's reign (2 Kings 19:30-31). But the presence of God's true Messiah – His own Son – is strongly suggested by Micah's expression *"like showers on the grass"* (verse 7), which is

---

* Other commentators also understand *"seven ... eight"* as an indefinite numerical sequence signifying 'many'.

'Thousands' (Micah 5:2)

Bethlehem, one of the most insignificant places in the whole of Judah, was the birthplace of King David, King Jesus, and possibly King Hezekiah ...

➤ The Hebrew word *eleph*, translated *"thousands"* in Micah 5:2, is the ordinary word for the number 1,000.

➤ Each tribe of Israel was divided into thousands of fighting men, each thousand having its own separate head (Numbers 1:16).

➤ The thousand continued to be a division of a tribe even after Israel were settled in Canaan (Joshua 22:21; 1 Samuel 10:19).

➤ A *"thousand"* became the term used to describe the smallest geographical or administrative unit in Israel (1 Samuel 23:23) – compare the English word 'hundred': "a subdivision of a British county or shire, having its own court" (OED).

➤ Both the NIV and the RSV translate *"thousands"* as *"clans"*.

➤ Gideon's 'thousand' was the *"weakest"* in Manasseh (Judges 6:15).

➤ The inhabitants of Bethlehem were so few in number that they were counted with those of neighbouring Netophah (Nehemiah 7:26).

"So lowly was Bethlehem that ... in the division under Joshua (Joshua 15), it was wholly omitted" (E.B. Pusey).

The *"Ruler ... whose goings forth are from of old, from everlasting"* (Micah 5:2)

What do the commentators say about the personal origins of the Messiah?

In favour of 'from eternity':

➤ "... the goings forth here ... are a going forth in eternity." (E.B. Pusey)

➤ "[The use of these terms] signifies that the origin of the future son of David would have a close connection with Yahweh Himself ... though the precise detail of the connection is not explained." (F.T. Pearce)

In favour of 'from the days of old' (the time of David):

➤ "... the prophecy refers to the whole dynasty of David from David himself to the scion of the moment or of the future." (J.H. Gailey)

➤ "... the advent of the new ruler ... will not be something newly conceived by God, but the fulfilment of something that began as far back as the monarchy began." (J. Marsh)

Reconciling the two views:

While the passage gives no grounds at all for the false notion that Jesus pre-existed personally 'from all eternity', these apparently conflicting views can be satisfactorily blended together. As the 'Logos' of John 1:1, conceived in the mind and purpose of God before the world existed in physical form, the Lord Jesus Christ came into the world for the first time as a real-life person in about 4 BC in Bethlehem. He was both *"the only-begotten Son of God"* and the Son of David, and as such he was heir to David's ancient throne. For Micah's contemporaries, therefore, this promised Messiah would understandably be thought of as 'King David revived' (as in Ezekiel 37:24-25). Yet the fulness of the meaning of Micah's prophecy can only be properly understood in the light of what the New Testament reveals about the Divine paternity of the Lord Jesus Christ.

almost certainly deliberately reminiscent of David's vision of the King-Messiah in Psalm 72:6: *"He shall come down like rain upon the mown grass, like showers that water the earth".* And Micah was clear, too, that none of this could be either helped or hindered by men (verse 7): it would all be the work of God.

But the second role of God's people at that time (whether under Hezekiah or Jesus) would be to sit in judgement over the nations, dominating them *"like a lion among the beasts of the forest"* and *"like a young lion among flocks of sheep",* with no-one to deliver (verse 8). From ancient times, the lion had been the emblem of the tribe of Judah (Genesis 49:9); so this was perhaps an echo of the role to be played by Jerusalem, which was likened earlier by Micah (in 4:13) to a beast with iron horns and bronze hooves. It would be a destroying, subjugating role, to be visited presumably on those who remained unaffected by the *"dew"* of Divine teaching and would not bow the knee in subjection to God's anointed (compare Psalm 2:8-12). And the work of God's people in those days was summarised by the lifting up of their hand against their *"adversaries"* and the cutting off of their *"enemies"* (verse 9).

5:10-15 – Getting rid of worldliness

Micah 5:10-15 is linked to the preceding picture of Messiah's people dispensing truth and justice to the nations by the phrase *"it shall be in that day"* (verse 10). But it quickly becomes clear that in order to fit them for such an important role, God Himself has first to purge His people of their worldliness. The urgent need to do this, and the sense of drama attached to God's work, is signified by His use of the first person singular *("I will …")* as He spoke about the things He was going to remove from His people so that they might learn to trust in Him alone.

The nation's enemies were to be *"cut off"* (verse 9). But before then, God would personally *"cut off"* the following things from His people:

- **Their *"horses"* (verse 10):** In spite of the fact that Israel's kings had been specifically commanded not to *"multiply horses … nor cause the people to return to Egypt to multiply horses"* (Deuteronomy 17:16), Solomon had done exactly that (1 Kings 10:25-29). In Micah's day, too, there was an abundance of horses in the land (Isaiah 2:7). Like the chariots with which horses were often associated, and which God would also *"destroy"* (verse 10), such (war)horses were generally a sign of trust in man's military might, rather than in the strength of God (see Isaiah 30:15,16, 31:1 and Psalm 20:7).

- **Their *"cities"* (verse 11):** Trust and confidence in fortified cities was not limited to the children of Israel. At about this same time, Isaiah was announcing the future fall of the king of Babylon by saying among other

Jesus as 'the peace' (Micah 5:5)

"The connections between Messiah and peace are numerous." (F.T. Pearce)

➤ Genesis 49:10 – *"The sceptre shall not depart from Judah, nor a law-giver from between his feet, until Shiloh ['The peaceful one'] comes; and to him shall be the obedience of the people."*

➤ 1 Kings 2:33 – *"… upon David and his descendants, upon his house and his throne, there shall be peace for ever from the LORD".*

➤ Psalm 72:7 – *"In his days the righteous shall flourish, and abundance of peace, until the moon is no more."*

➤ Isaiah 9:6 – *"And his name will be called … Prince of Peace."*

➤ Isaiah 53:5 – *"The chastisement for our peace was upon him, and by his stripes we are healed."*

➤ Zechariah 9:10 – *"He shall speak peace to the nations."*

➤ John 14:27 – *"Peace I leave with you, my peace I give to you."*

➤ Acts 10:36 – *"The word which God sent to the children of Israel, preaching peace through Jesus Christ."*

➤ Romans 5:1 – *"Therefore , having been justified by faith, we have peace with God through our Lord Jesus Christ."*

➤ Ephesians 2:14 – *"For he himself is our peace, who has made both one, and has broken down the middle wall of division between us."*

➤ Colossians 1:20 – *"… and by him to reconcile all things to himself … having made peace through the blood of his cross."*

➤ 1 Peter 5:14 – *"Peace to you all who are in Christ Jesus"*

"And this one shall be peace."

"There is no Messianic description with which we more readily or thankfully identify our Lord Jesus Christ." (R.F. Horton)

Seven shepherds?

Hezekiah's leading counsellors

Eliakim – Son of Hilkiah and Master of the royal household (2 Kings 18:18); approved by God, as a type of Jesus ("*a peg in a sure place*" – Isaiah 22:23).

Shebna – "*The scribe*", or Secretary (of State) (2 Kings 18:18) – a position to which he was demoted, having previously been Master of the household (Isaiah 22:15-19).

Joah – Son of Asaph and "*recorder*" (court record-keeper or historian – Isaiah 36:3).

Isaiah – Son of Amoz and court prophet (Isaiah 37:2).

In addition, mention is also made of "*the elders of the priests*" (for example in 2 Kings 19:2 and Isaiah 37:2). If there were three or four of these, then these seven or eight leading royal counsellors may well have been the (unnamed) "*seven shepherds (even) eight princely men*" of Micah 5:5.

things that he would no longer "*fill the face of the world with cities*" (Isaiah 14:21). Cities then, as now, tended also to become places of luxury, vice and crime – Sodom and Gomorrah had been legendary for such things. God was so determined to put an end to such worldly influences that He pronounced their doom a second and a third time: "*I will … throw down all your strongholds*" (verse 11 – compare Isaiah 2:15), and "*I will destroy your cities*" (verse 14);

- Their **"*sorceries*" (verse 12):** Pagan witchcraft was abominable to the God of Israel, and His people should have known better than to practise it (Deuteronomy 18:9-14). The command was clear: "*You shall have no soothsayers*" (the Hebrew word means, literally, 'observers of clouds'). Isaiah also reinforced the same message: the soothsayers simply had to be removed (Isaiah 2:6).

- Their **"*carved images*" and "*sacred pillars*" (verse 13):** The *pesel* (usually carved out of wood) and the *matstsebah* (almost always made of stone) were part of the equipment of idolatry, and God's people had been commanded to have nothing to do with them (Leviticus 26:1). They were the work of men's hands, and God would "*pluck*" them from their midst, together with all their *asherim* (the wooden posts representing Asherah, the wife of the Canaanite god Baal – verse 14). For a while at least, Hezekiah's reformation was to inspire God's people to get rid of these idols for themselves (2 Chronicles 31:1).

Then, when all these harmful things had been "*cut off*" from Israel, God would judge "*the nations that have not heard*" (the Hebrew word for "*heard*" would be better translated "*obeyed*", and this is more consistent with the righteous judgements of God being visited on the disobedient) (verse 15).

Questions on Part two (outline answers on page 67)

2.1 What were the three gifts that Micah claimed to have received from God, and why were they so important in his ministry?

2.2 What sin did the judges, priests and prophets in Judah all share in common, and how would Jesus have described this particular sin? (See Micah 3:11 and Luke 16:13)

2.3 Why were the people of Jerusalem so smugly sure that everything would be well with them?

2.4 In what sense might the picture painted in Micah 4:1,2 be thought of as 'the Tower of Babel in reverse' (Genesis 11:1-9)?

2.5 Why should *"dew"* and *"showers on the grass"* (5:7) be an appropriate image to represent the word of God and the teaching of Divine truth? (Isaiah 55:10,11 may be helpful.)

2.6 In general terms, what are our twenty-first century equivalents of horses, chariots, fortified cities, fortune-tellers, and images of wood and stone (5:10)?

8th century BC idols

"Your carved images I will also cut off ... you shall no more worship the work of your hands." (5:13)

Part three (6:1 to 7:20)

"HEAR NOW WHAT THE LORD SAYS … HEAR, O YOU MOUNTAINS"

> **(A) 6:1 TO 7:10: JUDGEMENT ON JUDAH AND JERUSALEM – THE GREAT ASSIZE COURT**

6:1-5 – God versus the people

It was Micah who announced the first case to be tried before the Divine court. He called the court to order to hear the case of God versus the people, and the jury, called on to witness the proceedings, consisted of "the great unchanging features of the earth, the mountains and the hills".* As witnesses to the original covenant between God and His people, which He was now accusing Judah of breaking, it was highly appropriate, and not at all unusual, that these permanent natural elements should be brought into play when the covenant was at stake (see for example Deuteronomy 4:26 and 31:28).

The legal language used reinforced the court procedure: *"plead your cause"*, *"the Lord's complaint"*, and *"He will contend* (margin: *"bring charges against")* His

> * Fred Pearce, *From Hosea to Zephaniah*, op.cit., page 146.

people". In verses 3-5, it was the Lord God Himself (Yahweh) who began His case against His people with a couple of pointed personal questions and an invitation (verse 3):

- *"What have I done to you?"*
- *"How have I wearied you?"* (Isaiah 43:22-24 contains similar language).
- *"Testify against Me"* – make your defence, if you can (compare Isaiah 43:26).

There was no adequate answer to such questions. God's people had tired of Him, but they had no real reasons for doing so. By contrast, God had done everything possible for them, as the Exodus had clearly demonstrated:

- God had brought them up *"from the land of Egypt"* (verse 4).
- He had redeemed them *"from the house of bondage"* (verse 4).
- He had sent *"Moses, Aaron and Miriam"* to lead them (verse 4).
- He had turned Balaam's curses into a blessing (verse 5).
- He had brought them safely across the Jordan – from *"Acacia Grove"* (i.e.

Shittim, the last stopping-place before the entry of God's people into the land, where the people committed idolatry – Numbers 25:1) *"to Gilgal"*, the place of their first encampment in Canaan (Joshua 5), where the males were all circumcised and a new beginning was made (verse 5).

In all this, God had acted in mercy towards His people, and they had had every opportunity to *"know the righteousness of the LORD"* (verse 5).

6:6-8 – Spokesman for the defence: What does God want?

At this point in the courtroom drama, the spokesman for the defence stepped forward. But he made no attempt to justify Judah's waywardness, and offered no defence. Instead, he humbly accepted the justice of God's complaint and made a sincere enquiry about the best way back to God both for himself and for the nation. The question was, in effect: 'How could an individual, or a whole nation, restore a relationship with God that was broken because of sin?'

And if, as suggested in these pages, the spokesman really was Hezekiah, then this (rightly) famous question about the best way back to God takes on an added layer of meaning as the young king asked:

> *"With what shall I come before the LORD, and bow myself before the High God?"* (verse 6)

Poised to take over the governance of God's people, here was a young man at a crucial decision-point in his life. He had been brought up to think that animal sacrifices and *"rivers of oil"* were what God wanted from His people (verses 6,7). As a young boy, he had perhaps seen the large-scale sacrificial slaughtering and burning in which his father Ahaz indulged (2 Kings 16:12-15). So was this the kind of thing that God wanted? Did He really expect the sacrifice of children, such as Ahaz had offered (2 Kings 16:3), *"the fruit of my body for the sin of my soul"?* (verse 7). Did the Lord want more of that from Hezekiah? What should the young king do to obtain the forgiveness of the nation's sin?

And it was here, at what must have been a defining moment in Micah's own ministry, as well as in the life of Hezekiah and the nation, that the prophet himself was inspired to reply on behalf of God to the genuine appeal of a young man seeking God. And the prophet did it by uttering one of the most sublime and enduring sentences in the whole of recorded scripture:

> *"(God) has shown you, O man, what is good; and what does the LORD require of you but to do justly, to love mercy and to walk humbly with your God?"* (verse 8)

God had shown all the children of Israel, including Hezekiah, in His righteous laws, exactly how He wanted them to behave in daily life. The essence of the Divine law had been written down for them to read 500 years before, in language almost identical to Micah's:

> *"And now, Israel, what does the* Lord *your God require of you, but to fear the* Lord *your God, to walk in all his ways and to love him, to serve the* Lord *your God with all your heart and with all your soul, and to keep the commandments of the* Lord *and his statutes which I command you today for your good."*
>
> (Deuteronomy 10:12,13)

But by the time of Micah, Israel in general had lost sight of all this. They had come to think only in terms of external rituals and giving God physical things – as if the Maker of heaven and earth actually needed anything material that they could give back to Him out of all the substance with which He had blessed them. Like the Pharisees in the days of the Lord Jesus, God's people in the time of Micah had failed to understand the spiritual lessons of the Law. They had *"neglected the weightier matters of the law: justice, mercy and faith"* (Matthew 23:23). Yet here stood a young man before the Lord, newly elevated to the leadership of God's people, willing to stand as their spokesman and ready to take responsibility for their sin (see 2 Chronicles 29:5-11).

Hezekiah was prepared to listen to the prophet's advice and to make it the guiding principle of his life: his subsequent prayer for his people (*"May the good* Lord *provide atonement for everyone who prepares his heart to seek God, the* Lord *God of his fathers"* – 2 Chronicles 30:18-19) shows how very seriously he received the Divine instruction. In this, too, the young king foreshadowed yet again his own greater son who, above all men, was to display the true significance of Micah 6:8 in his perfect life of justice, mercy and humble faith. The thing that God required most of all was the kind of living sacrifice of which His Son Jesus would be the prime example: the humility of one who would put God's way first in his life rather than his own.

But if Hezekiah had now been personally directed in the way he should go, the courtroom drama still had to be concluded, and God's complaints were not yet over! God still had a case to bring against the city of Jerusalem; and so the remainder of the chapter is taken up with God's accusation against the wickedness in the city (verses 9-12) and by His judicial sentence of punishment to come (verses 13-16).

6:9-12 – God versus Jerusalem

God continued His formal complaints, and spoke through the prophet in loud reproach against *"the city"* (verse 9). Jerusalem had already received plenty of warning and instruction about its behaviour: since at least the time of Solomon (almost 300 years before), the voice of wisdom had been crying out to the inhabitants of the city (see Proverbs 8:1-3) to tell them that *"The fear of the* Lord *is the beginning of wisdom"* (Proverbs 9:10). And now that same *"voice"* was telling them again that *"Wisdom shall*

"Do justly ... love mercy ... walk humbly with your God" (Micah 6:8)

These three requirements highlight precisely what it was that Judah and the inhabitants of Jerusalem were failing to do. Their actions, their attitude, and their relationship with God were all wrong, and these were the three antidotes to their failure.

➤ The first requirement was to *"do justly"*, or to practise just judgement. The Hebrew word *mishpat* is a legal word (like much of the language in Micah) and it occurs throughout the Law of Moses. It means right judgement and is associated with the verdict of a court once all the evidence has been weighed and the truth has been established. It is closely bound up with God's own nature, and with His righteousness, which can never allow Him to do wrong. To *"do justly"*, therefore, is to imitate God's behaviour by making only appropriate decisions, guided by the laws of God. If the children of Israel could do that, it would mean that they would help, rather than oppress and rob, the needy; they would have a bias towards the poor; and they would house the homeless, provide for the widows and orphans, be honest in their trading and commerce, and be generous to the stranger in their midst. All these actions were essential parts of what the law of God required in human relationships (Deuteronomy 24:17-22).

➤ Closely associated with this proper sense of justice was the second Divine requirement: *"to love mercy"*, or to love with kindness. The Hebrew word *chesed* is most often expressive of the love – the loyalty – shown by God to those who are in covenant with Him, and it can be translated as covenant love, or covenant loyalty. It was one of the principal attributes of God revealed to Moses on Mount Sinai (Exodus 34:7), and it is mentioned again by Micah in his closing Psalm of praise (7:18). If Israel were to show this unswerving loyalty towards the God they had all once solemnly promised faithfully to serve, then they would need a change of attitude: instead of loving themselves in so many selfish ways which resulted in unkindness to others, they would need to concentrate on loving (being loyal to) God, as the Law of Moses required (Deuteronomy 6:5).

➤ The third part of this integrated trio of requirements was *"to walk humbly with your God"*, or to *"humble thyself to walk"* with God, as the AV margin puts it. The Hebrew word *tsana* occurs only here; but the meaning is clear. It has to do with maintaining an appropriate relationship with God, by recognising His supremacy, and by returning His loving care with faithful devotion. 'Walking humbly with God', therefore, is to share the loving fellowship that the Lord Jesus enjoyed with His Father, remembering always that even the Son of God recognised His Father's pre-eminence in all things (John 14:28). And, if the Jews of Micah's day were to be restored to such a close personal relationship with their God, it would mean that they would have to stop walking *"haughtily"* as Micah saw them doing (2:3), and get back to obeying *"the first and great commandment"* of the Law (Matthew 22:37,38).

"So, in the courtroom scene Israel has been shown that God does not require the sacrifice of rams, or the pouring out of oil, sacrifices from outside a person, but the yielding of a total life to God in God's own way. What is required is the conforming of a life to God's own life … It is a pilgrimage both with God and to God" (Mary Tanner).

see [the Hebrew word is the word for 'fear'] *Your name"* (verse 9).[1] And those who feared God's Name would know that *"the Rod"* (the Assyrians – Isaiah 10:5) had already been *"appointed"* by God (verse 9). Jerusalem's punishment was sure to come because:

- The homes of the wicked were full of ill-gotten riches (*"the treasures of wickedness",* verse 10).

- People were cheating in business, giving *"short measure"* (literally: 'an epha of leanness' – i.e. it was less than the standard size), with *"wicked* (that is, inaccurate) *balances"* and *"deceitful weights"* (verses 10,11).

- God was unable to regard His people as *"pure"* because of all their dishonesty (verse 11).

- The rich would stop at nothing (including violence) to gain their ends (verse 12).

- The place was full of lying and falsehood (verse 12).

And all of this was in direct contravention of God's law, set out clearly in Leviticus 19:35,36 and Deuteronomy 25:13-16.

6:13-16 – The sentence of the Judge

The court proceedings were brought to an end with the judicial sentence on the wickedness of the inhabitants of Jerusalem. The sentence itself was introduced in verse 13 by the linking word *"therefore",* and the punishment would consist of several elements:

- Jerusalem's inhabitants would be struck down with incurable diseases[2] and wounds (the same language is used in Nahum 3:19) (verse 13).

- They would be continually hungry (verse 14).

- Whatever they hoarded would be taken away violently (verse 14).

- They would sow, but not reap (verse 15).

- They would make olive oil, but never use it (verse 15).

- They would make wine, but never drink it (verse 15).

- They would be made *"a desolation"* (margin: *"an object of horror"*), and other people would *"hiss"* at their *"reproach"* (verse 16).

These punishments for disobedience were all legally appropriate: they were

---

1 – The Revised Standard Version translates this sentence: "… *it is sound wisdom to fear thy Name".*

2 – It is just possible that this is a reference to the fatal disease which struck Hezekiah (2 Kings 20:1) from which God cured him on account of his faithful prayer.

included in the curses for disobedience laid out by Moses in Deuteronomy 28 (especially verses 15-48), and were part of the solemn covenant into which the children of Israel had entered with God. The curses would come on Judah because, like Israel, they had adopted the wicked ways and practices which were current in the days of Omri and Ahab (verse 16). To *"walk in their counsels"*, rather than in the ways of God, was exactly the opposite of what God required (verse 8). Instead of justice, mercy and a humble walking with God, there was the evil, selfish and violent lifestyle of two of Israel's most wicked kings.

7:1-10 – The defendant's lament and confession

It's not at all obvious from the text itself whether the court scene ended with chapter 6, or whether the lament that followed in chapter 7:1-10 (or perhaps even the whole of chapter 7) should be seen as an integral part of the formal judicial proceedings. The pronouncement of the guilty verdict and the sentence of punishment that followed it in chapter 6 were so devastating that it is natural to see the lament as a direct reaction to the courtroom drama. **But whose reaction was it?** Most commentators interpret the 10-verse lament as if these were the words of the prophet, sorrowing at the bleak prospect ahead for the people and the city of God, both of which had been roundly condemned by their God in chapter 6. But it seems perfectly possible that the lament was

actually an expression of Hezekiah's personal distress at the Divine Judge's condemnation of Judah and Jerusalem which he had just heard.

Understood in that light, the lament shows the young king pouring out his sorrow in the following terms:

- **verse 1:** He expressed his misery first with a heart-rending cry of woe reminiscent of Job (10:15) and Isaiah (Isaiah 6:5).

- **verse 1:** He likened himself to a disappointed fruit-farmer who, coming into his orchard in the early summertime (when any first-ripe fruit would be at its sweetest – Isaiah 28:4) found no fruit on either his vine or his fig tree, thus acknowledging that God could find no good works among His people. This was an image which looked forward to the parable of the barren fig tree in Luke 13:6-9; and it serves to reinforce the parallels between Hezekiah and the Lord Jesus, who was also sad to have to recognise the failure of Israel to bring *"fruits worthy of repentance"* to God.

- **verses 2,3:** He readily admitted that none of his contemporaries had remained *"faithful"* (margin: *"loyal"*) to the national covenant with God. There was no-one *"upright among men"* – they were all violent, doing evil *"with both hands"*. Isaiah was also saying the same thing: *"The righteous*

perishes, and no man takes it to heart" (Isaiah 57:1).

- **verses 3,4:** Hezekiah felt a sense of isolation: he was surrounded by corrupt princes and judges, and by eminent people who were continually devising evil, plotting together, and taking bribes (which was specifically against the Law of Moses – Deuteronomy 16:19). Even the best of them was *"like a brier"* or a *"thorn hedge"* (compare 2 Samuel 23:6); and they all fully deserved the coming day of judgement and of *"perplexity"* that had been pronounced by their *"watchman"* – perhaps the prophet Micah in this context.

- **verses 5,6:** He was living in a time of social breakdown, when the ties of friendship and kinship were severely damaged. Even the closest friend, companion, or wife, might be capable of letting you down or betraying you. Sons were turning against fathers, daughters against mothers, and daughters-in-law against mothers-in-law. Even the members of your own household could turn out to be your enemies. Yet another parallel between Hezekiah and Christ is suggested by the fact that these two verses were quoted by Jesus in Matthew 10:35-36, where he applied them directly to his own situation. Like his Father in Deuteronomy 32:15, the Lord Jesus was dishonoured by his earthly family.

- **verse 7:** The only person he could really trust was God Himself; so he resolved to look to Him, and to *"wait"* for Him, confident that God at least would hear and save him from his distress.

It really is very striking how almost all that Hezekiah spoke of here applied also to the earthly life of the Lord Jesus. So much so, in fact, that it helps us gain valuable insights into the difficulties faced by both men – including their sense of isolation – when performing such responsible tasks against a background of opposition, immorality and wickedness.

The parallels continued, with Hezekiah advising his *"enemy"* not to gloat over his apparent downfall. Even if he fell, he would rise again; even when he sat *"in darkness"*, his God would *"be a light"* to him (verse 8). This was a foretaste, surely, of the confidence of the Lord Jesus that his Father would raise him from the dead. Hezekiah also accepted the justice of God's judgement against him on account of his own sin; but he still had faith that God would *"plead"* his case in His righteousness and would bring him out into the light once more (verse 9). (The Lord Jesus himself had no personal sins, of course; but the Apostle Paul tells us that Jesus *"who knew no sin"* was *"made … to be sin for us"* (2 Corinthians 5:21); so perhaps Micah 7:9 can be understood to apply to the Lord Jesus in that particular sense.)

As for Hezekiah, he looked forward in faith to the time when the *"enemy"* who had mocked him by asking *"Where is the LORD your God?"* would be ashamed, and when he would see *"her"* trampled under foot like *"mire in the streets"* (verse 10). It's not at all clear why this *"enemy"* is personified as female. We don't know enough about Hezekiah's private life to be able to identify a particular woman who mocked his personal faith in God. But the female enemy here may just be an ironic personification of the power of Assyria, or perhaps even the Assyrian capital city, Nineveh.

Assyria, represented in 2 Kings 18:32-35 by Sennacherib's envoy Rabshakeh, certainly mocked Hezekiah's reliance and trust in God in exactly these terms. For his part, the Lord Jesus Christ was similarly mocked while he was hanging on the cross: *"He trusted in God; let him deliver him now …"* (Matthew 27:43).

(B) 7:11-20: ULTIMATE DELIVERANCE FOR GOD'S PEOPLE

7:11-13 – Jerusalem rebuilt and repopulated

The Lord God Himself made a direct response to Hezekiah's lament and confession. The prophecy was addressed, through Micah, to the city of Jerusalem (*"your walls"* are mentioned in verse 11) – but this may be because Hezekiah had taken the sins of the city upon himself in standing as its spokesman. And it was in

response to Hezekiah's humility and intercession that the message from God now turned to one of deliverance and of hope for the future:

- **verse 11:** The walls of Jerusalem would one day be built up again (the word for *"walls"* here signifies 'hedges' rather than defensive fortifications, and suggests a time of peace rather than of war – there would then be no need for the *"strongholds"* of 5:11).

- **verse 11:** *"In that day"* the nation's boundaries would be widely extended (this is based on the alternative translation in the margin, and seems preferable to the idea of a *"decree"* going out).

- **verse 12:** *"In that day"* also, people would come to Jerusalem from Assyria and from the cities of Egypt (see the margin). They would come from all over the known world: from the South (*"the fortress"* = Egypt, as in the Revised Version), from the North (*"the River"* = Hebrew *nahar*, the Euphrates, as in Genesis 15:18), and from both the West and the East (*"from sea* [the Mediterranean] *to sea"* [the Persian Gulf – see Joel 2:20]). They would come, too, *"from mountain to mountain"*, which may mean from Sinai in the South to Lebanon in the North. But the idea conveyed is comprehensive: **very many people** (perhaps in the first instance, the Jews taken captive by the Assyrians, and those who had fled for safety into other lands)[1] **would come to Jerusalem and help to repopulate the city of God**.

- **verse 13:** For a time, however, *"the land"* (or perhaps *"the earth"?*) itself would be *"desolate"*. This was one of the punishments God had said would follow disobedience – Leviticus 26:33; see also Isaiah 6:11) until it had been cleansed of the wickedness of those who had previously lived there. Like Hezekiah, God had looked for *"the first-ripe fruit"* (7:1), but had found only *"the fruit of their (mis)deeds"*.

The multiple applications of these verses should not be overlooked. The return of large numbers of captives to Judah, from Assyria and elsewhere, must have been an awesome thing in itself;[2] and no doubt it served to vindicate Micah and Isaiah, both of whom had foretold the event (compare Micah 7:11,12 with Isaiah 11:11,12).

And yet both prophets seem to have been pointing even further forward, to the day when not only exiled Jews would return in large numbers to their ancient land, but when people of *"many nations"* (Micah 4:2;

Isaiah says, *"all nations"* – Isaiah 2:2) would go up to the house of God in Jerusalem, as foreseen by Micah in one of his earlier prophecies about "the latter days" (4:1).

Once again, then, we find clear evidence here of the events of Hezekiah's reign providing both a primary fulfilment of Micah's words and a foretaste of a greater fulfilment still to come.

7:14,15 – The prophet's prayer and the Divine response

This Divine promise of deliverance served to prompt the grateful prophet to pray fervently for that day to come soon. And so Micah pleaded with God (verse 14),

- To come and play the part of a shepherd once more.
- To rule His people again with His *"staff"* (the Hebrew word means a 'sceptre', suggesting kingship).
- To treat them as *"the flock"* of His *"heritage"* (compare Deuteronomy 9:26 and Psalm 95:7 – God's people **belonged** to Him).
- To *"let them feed"* once again, not in solitary wooded hills like those in distant Carmel, but together in the

---

1 – "Naturally enough, when the invading armies began to pour across the borders of Israel and Judah, many would flee for refuge to one of the nearby territories (hence such verses as Isaiah 11:11)." Harry Whittaker, *Hezekiah the Great,* op.cit., page 86.

2 – Harry Whittaker suggests that there may have been more than 200,000 captives who returned from Assyria in the time of Hezekiah. Ibid., pages 85,86.

luxuriant pastures of Bashan and Gilead on the East of Jordan. They had fed there *"in the days of old"*; but the territory had been lost to the Assyrians during the reign of Ahaz (2 Kings 15:29).

And Micah's prayer did not go unheard, for his reference to the *"days of old"* prompted God's immediate response (verse 15). Picking up Micah's words, the Lord remembered the great days of the Exodus, and made a solemn promise to do miracles on behalf of His people like those He performed when He brought them out of Egypt and into the land of promise (Exodus 34:10).

7:16-20 – The nations humbled and God's promises fulfilled: *"Who is like Yah?"*

To this good news, Micah responded prophetically, with an up-beat enthusiasm that lasted until the very last verse of this written version of his prophecies. The Lord God, he said, would make the nations that had brought such distress on Israel experience shame and humiliation, accompanied by both dumbness and deafness (verse 16). Like the serpent in Eden (Genesis 3:14), they would *"lick the dust"* as a sign of their humiliation; they would desert their fortifications recognising that they were powerless against the awesome strength of the Almighty; and they would come to learn the fear of the Lord the hard way (verse 17).

Awestruck too by the reminder of God's supreme power, Micah felt compelled to break into praise. Reflecting on the meaning of his own name ('Who is like Yah?'), he played on it by asking: *"Who is a God like you …?"*. His question was borrowed from the song of praise that Moses sang after the great deliverance from Egypt (Exodus 15:11), and Exodus 34 provided part of the answer to the question. So Micah quoted a few verses (Exodus 34:6,7), where the Name of the Lord was explained to Moses:

> *"Pardoning iniquity and passing over … transgression … he does not retain his anger forever, because he delights in mercy."* (verse 18)

The greatness of God resides as much as anything in His moral attributes; so Micah concluded that God would genuinely forgive His people's wrongdoings and would cast all their sins *"into the depths of the sea"* (verse 19).

And the most fitting conclusion of all to the record of Micah's ministry and message? It came in the form of a happy and confident remembrance of the age-old and changeless promises of God to Abraham and the fathers of the nation. There could surely be no higher note of assurance and of hope on which to end any book of prophecy:

> *"You will give truth to Jacob and mercy to Abraham, which you have sworn to our fathers from days of old."* (verse 20)

Like those of David (2 Samuel 23:1), the words of Micah, the faithful prophet of the Lord, were ended …

Questions on Part three (outline answers on page 68)

3.1 There are four examples of legal words in Micah 6:1-3. Can you find them and say why it was appropriate for Micah to use such language in this particular context?

3.2 How does Micah 6:6-8 show us that God is more interested in what's inside us than what's outside us?

3.3 Why should justice and mercy be so important to us in our relationship with other people?

3.4 In Micah 7:1-10 there are at least seven points of comparison between Hezekiah's experiences and the life of Jesus. How many of them can you identify?

3.5 God's devastating power is depicted in Micah 7:16-17 in terms of its effect on the nations (*"ashamed" ... "hand over their mouth" ... "deaf" ... "lick the dust" ... "crawl from their holes"*). What kind of warfare does this make you think of? (Look at Zechariah 14:12-15 for an even more graphic description of how God will punish those who fight against Jerusalem at the Second Coming of Jesus.)

3.6 What is our equivalent of the Exodus from Egypt in terms of what God has done and will do for us?

Micah for today

> "The challenges and hopes of Micah ...
> are not dead history. They belong to
> us, and we have to make them alive for
> our world."   (J.I. Alfaro)

WHILE Micah spoke strongly and firmly to his contemporaries, for perhaps as long as 40 years, his prophecies were full, not only of searching criticisms of the sins of those to whom he spoke, but also of warnings and promises about things which would happen in the future. And all his messages were centred on unchanging principles, based on the justice and righteousness of God. Unlike His wayward people, God Himself never changes (Malachi 3:6). Micah's words, therefore, while grounded in the 8th-century BC historical context of the prophet's lifetime, have a timeless quality which makes his ministry continually relevant for all those, in every age, who try to serve God by allowing Divine principles to become the dominant influence in their lives.

A careful analysis of the 105 verses of Micah's recorded words reveals that there are at least 30 issues in Micah's prophecy that are still relevant today for those who claim to be the people of God.

In chapter 1, Micah talks about the coming judgements of God (verse 13), the need for repentance and reformation (verse 10) and the transgressions of God's people (verse 13).

In chapter 2, he speaks of the dangers of covetousness (verse 2), restricting the Spirit of God (verse 2), living in an evil time (verse 3), the need to let God's word affect our lives (verse 7), the importance of personal trustworthiness (verse 8), taking away the glory of God (verse 9), and the sin of lying (verse 11).

In chapter 3, he says that God will hide His face from those whose deeds are evil (verse 4), that we should not be partial in our judgements (verse 11), that we should not assume that just because we are the people of God, we cannot be harmed (verse 11), and that we should be acutely conscious of God's uniqueness and all-powerfulness (verse 18).

In chapter 4, he counsels us to have a love for the things of God (verse 2), to walk in God's Name (verse 5), and to long for the coming of our King (verse 9).

In **chapter 5**, he teaches us the need to recognise the sovereignty of our Messiah (verses 2-5), to behave towards others as 'dew from the Lord' (verse 7), and not to rely on material things, as a modern form of idolatry (verses 10-14).

In **chapter 6**, he makes us consider whether God might have a reasonable complaint against us (verse 2), whether we find the service of God wearisome (verse 3), whether we are conscious of the great things that God has done for us (verses 4,5), whether our lives reflect what God wants from us (verse 8), whether we understand the personal implications of the Name of God (verse 9 – an issue which is expanded in chapter 7:18,19), whether we are honest in all our dealings (verses 10,11), and whether we might be keeping the evil statutes of Omri, one of Israel's most wicked kings (verse 16).

And finally, **in chapter 7**, Micah asks us if we're saddened that natural Israel is still fruitless (verse 1), if other people are able to rely on us as a faithful friend (verse 5), if we look only to God for our salvation (verse 7), and if we're genuinely hoping for the fulfilment of God's promises to Abraham (verse 20).

These telling points make a long list; and they represent helpful personal reminders of what God always looks for from those who are His. And we can make Micah's words even more directly relevant for us in our twenty-first century lives by turning all the prophet's points into a checklist of searching questions.

Just read through the questions below and try to answer them honestly for yourself, and you'll soon see how very much **Micah is a prophet for today**:

- What difference does it make to your life to know that the judgement of God is coming on the earth? (1:3)
- What practical effect does the need for personal repentance and reformation have on your life? (1:10)
- How conscious are you of your personal transgressions? (1:13)
- Do you covet any of the things that other people have? (2:2)
- Are you conscious of living in an evil time – and what is your attitude to the things that you see going on around you? (2:3)
- Do you ever doubt the power of God? (2:7)
- Do you allow God's word to affect your life for the better? (2:7)
- Are you personally trustworthy? (2:8)
- Are you guilty of 'taking away' the glory of God? (2:9)
- Do you ever tell lies? (2:11)
- Does it matter to you that God will hide his face from you when you do wrong? (3:4)
- Are you partial in the judgements you make about other people? (3:11)

- Do you think that because you are one of God's people you can never come to any harm? (3:11)
- Are you genuinely aware of God's uniqueness and all-powerfulness? (3:18)
- Do you love the things of God and take every opportunity to learn more about Him? (4:2)
- Do you walk in God's Name? (4:5)
- How much do you long for the coming of your King? (4:9)
- In what ways does your life reflect your recognition of the sovereignty of your Messiah? (5:2-5)
- Do you behave like 'dew from the Lord'? (5:7)
- What kind of idols play an important part in your life? (5:10-14)
- Could God have a reasonable complaint about certain aspects of your life? (6:2)
- Do you ever find God's service wearisome? (6:3)
- Are you always conscious of the great things that God has done for you? (6:4,5)
- Are justice, mercy and humility the defining characteristics of your life? (6:8)
- Are you honest in your dealings with other people? (6:10,11)
- Do any evil principles (like "the statutes of Omri" – 6:16) govern any of your behaviour?

- Does it sadden you that natural Israel has not yet brought any fruit to God? (7:1)
- Are you a reliable friend and companion, or do you sometimes let others down? (7:5)
- Do you look only to God for your salvation? (7:7)
- Is the fulfilment of the promises of God to Abraham a central part of your hope for the future? (7:20)

Your answers to all these searching questions from Micah should serve to bring Micah's teaching into stark relief in a twenty-first century context. But in case some of the expressions Micah used seem a bit obscure, you might like to try doing a little Bible study of your own by looking through the panel of supplementary questions on the next page.

And when you've done that, just ask yourself how you think you measure up against Micah's penetrating criticisms:

- Could God have a complaint against you as He did against Israel and Judah? And if so, what are you going to do about it?
- But don't be depressed! Just bear in mind how positively the young King Hezekiah reacted to Micah's message:

"Did he not fear the Lord and seek the Lord's favour? And the Lord relented concerning the doom which He had pronounced against them."

(Jeremiah 26:19)

Supplementary questions – an opportunity for Bible study on your own (outline answers on page 68)

1. Can you name some of the *"transgressions of Israel"* that were found in *"the daughter of Zion"* (1:13)? [Clue: Look at the panel on Lachish (page 20) and at Micah 2:1,2,8,9.]

2. In what way might it be possible to restrict the Spirit of the Lord (2:7)? [Clue: How did Micah's hearers react to his God-given prophecies (see 2:6)? The contemporaries of Jesus were guilty of exactly the same thing (John 5:37-39).]

3. How do we all take away (or fall short of) "the glory of God" (2:9)? [Clue: Look at Romans 3:23 in its context.]

4. What does 'walking in God's Name' (4:5) mean in practical terms? [Clue: Read Micah 7:18,19 carefully, then compare it with Exodus 34:5-7, where God's Name was proclaimed to Moses, and translate those Divine characteristics into ways of behaving in daily life.]

5. What is *"dew from the Lord"* a symbol of (5:7)? [Clue: The context in Micah 5:7 ought to help, as well as Deuteronomy 32:2 and Psalm 72:6.]

6. Why were Judah's horses, chariots, sorceries, soothsayers and cities regarded by God as unacceptable to Him as their carved images and sacred pillars (5:10-14)? [Clue: We are guilty of the same thing if we rely on material things more than on God. See 1 Corinthians 10:14.]

7. God denied wearying His people (6:3). But how did Israel's weariness with the things of God cause God Himself to become weary of them? [Clue: The answer is to be found somewhere in Isaiah 43.]

8. What were *"the statutes of Omri"* (6:16)? [Clue: Omri's reign is summarised in 1 Kings 16:21-28.]

9. When will natural Israel bring fruit to God (7:1)? [Clue: The answer is embedded in what the apostle Paul has to say in Romans 11:15-27.]

10. What did God actually promise to Abraham (7:20)? [Clue: There are nine things promised to Abraham in Genesis 12:2,3,7; 13:14-17; 15:4,5,18; 17:1-8,15-21; 21:12,13; 22:15-18.]

Micah for tomorrow

"The eighth century prophets were fiercely obsessed with the future."
(B.W. Anderson)

FROM a purely human point of view, Micah proclaimed his message in a political situation which provided no real ground for confidence in the nation's survival. Precariously located between the superpowers of Mesopotamia in the north and Egypt in the south, Israel and Judah were very much in the firing line. They were trapped in a seemingly hopeless situation, with powerful opposing forces looking certain to crush them as they marched towards world domination.

But Micah's messages were not all gloomy. In common with the messages of the other true prophets of God, Micah's pessimistic pronouncements about the doom of God's people were also heavily tinged with optimism for the longer-term. We can see this clearly from the two tables which follow and which illustrate the dramatic contrast between the near-term fate of Jerusalem in Micah 3 and the *"latter days"* vision of deliverance and restoration in Micah 4.

The destruction of Jerusalem, graphically prophesied in Micah 3, was deferred thanks to Hezekiah's timely reformation. But a century or so later in 586 BC, the task which Sennacherib the Assyrian had begun was completed when Jerusalem was sacked by the Babylonians.

Fall of the old Jerusalem (Micah 3)
"Now" – in the time of Micah (3:9)
Temple Mount to be laid bare (3:12)
Leaders corrupt (3:9,11)
Zion built on bloodshed and crime (3:10)
Leaders taking bribes and practising injustice (3:11)
People leaning complacently on the Lord (3:11)
Zion to be violently removed (3:12)

Further fulfilments of those same words of doom came even later under the Romans in AD 70 and AD 135. Yet apart from that tiny foretaste of future glory in the closing years of Hezekiah's reign, thousands of years have passed without the fulfilment of the scenes of Zion's triumph and of Messiah's reign that Micah painted in chapter 4 especially. But with the eye of faith Micah saw those days coming; and he still remains very much, for us, a prophet of hope for our own tomorrow.

The work of Israel's Messiah and the long-term ministry of the world's Saviour and anointed King, Jesus Christ, are an ever-present theme in Micah's prophecies. The humble birth of Jesus in Bethlehem, his tears over Jerusalem, the power that filled him by the Spirit of the Lord, his outspokenness against the greed and violence of the scribes and Pharisees, his humiliation at the hands of wicked men, his position as the great shepherd of the sheep, and all the many ways in which his life was prefigured in the life of Hezekiah – all these Messianic insights are found in Micah (see table opposite).

Even more, reaching out to our own *"latter days"* and beyond, Micah had much to say about the Lord's work at his Second Coming, in three key passages which provide a fitting conclusion to this study of Micah's prophecy. The passages are typical of Micah's longer-term view of Israel's national Messiah – a prospect which, in its latter-day aspects, has much to teach us about what is still to happen in the purpose of God.

Micah 2:12,13 – This prophecy came immediately after the judgements pronounced against Israel and Judah, and

Deliverance of the new Jerusalem (Micah 4)
"In the latter days" (4:1)
Mountain of the Lord's house to be exalted (4:1)
Zion to become the head (4:1)
Zion to be the centre of Divine teaching (4:2)
The Lord to administer proper justice (4:3)
Genuine worship of the Lord (4:5)
No more war (4:3-4)

which came to pass within 20 years at most, when first Shalmaneser and Sargon invaded the land of the northern tribes, and then Sennacherib conquered the greater part of Judah. Immediately after the last of these Assyrian invasions, Judah and Jerusalem – delivered for the time being from any further threat – enjoyed a period of peace and blessing under Hezekiah.

Micah 2:12,13, speaking of a Divine deliverance from the destruction of a besieging enemy, was therefore fulfilled initially in the lifetime of the prophet; and this would be compelling evidence of the prophet's authenticity according to Jeremiah's test:

> *"The prophet who prophesies of peace, when the word of the prophet*

comes to pass, the prophet will be known as one whom the Lord has truly sent." (28:9)

But the events surrounding King Sennacherib's abortive siege of Jerusalem were only typical of things still to happen in the latter days. Throughout Micah the Lord Jesus is represented as the shepherd of Israel; and in these verses of deliverance it's the Spirit of Christ which speaks as God through the prophet about a great future gathering of the lost sheep of Israel: *"I will surely assemble all of you, O Jacob. I will surely gather the remnant of Israel; I will put them together like sheep of the fold, like a flock in the midst of their pasture".* And the one who, in his first coming to men, revealed the moral attributes – the personal glory – of the Father, will, in his second coming, manifest the Lord God in all His power, and will carry out the Divine purpose with no possibility of successful human opposition.

In that day it will be truly said: *"The one who breaks open will come up before them … their king will pass before them, with the* Lord *at their head"* (Micah 2:13). And whatever historical precedents there may have been for this yet future event, this picture of *"the one who breaks open"* can only be properly understood in its fulness as a prophecy about the Lord Jesus in his military role as the defender of God's people and as the scourge of their enemies in the latter days.

Micah 4:1-5:15 – These Messianic verses of promised deliverance and vengeance are among the best loved parts of scripture. It's possible to see, in the golden years of Hezekiah's extended reign, many foretastes of the wonderful age of righteousness of Messiah's kingdom. But even the high points of Hezekiah's time of blessing were only a dim approximation of the glory that is yet to be revealed in Israel. To Micah fell the honour of painting some of the clearest and most vivid pictures of the establishment of the kingdom of God on earth. A straightforward reading of these two chapters should fill us with renewed zeal for the coming of the day of the Lord.

Yet the sequence of passages in these chapters of hope is not easy to grasp, since the overall picture of the fortunes of Israel down the ages to the kingdom is not presented in a simple chronological order. Chapter 4 begins with a picture of the kingdom established, with *"the Lord's house"* established *"on the top of the mountains"* and providing a central place of worship for all nations, like that foreseen by Isaiah (56:7). Verses 9-11 seem to revert back to the Babylonian captivity (even though it was still future in Micah's time); but verses 12 and 13 repeat the promise of latter-day deliverance. (Chapter 5:1 strictly belongs to this promise: it is part of chapter 4 in the Hebrew Bible.) The birth of Messiah is promised in the early verses of chapter 5; but the chapter then seems to jump over almost 2,000 years of what is now history to the time of Messiah's victory over his people's enemies ("*He shall stand and feed his flock in the strength of the* LORD" – verse 4).

The explanation for this apparently random time-sequence is almost certainly bound up with some preliminary fulfilment in the life of Hezekiah – "*... this one shall be peace. When the Assyrian comes into our land*" (verse 5). But the promise again goes far beyond even that great monarch's achievements, for God has pledged to cleanse the land for ever, and to "*execute vengeance in anger and fury on the nations that have not heard*" (verse 15). Like Micah, and the faithful in his day, we too look in faith for the coming of the one who is to be "*Ruler in Israel, whose goings forth are from old, from everlasting*" (verse 2), and who will subdue and destroy the latter-day Assyrian (whoever controls present-day Iraq?) at the time of Christ's coming.

Micah 7:11-20 – Whether we are alive when it happens or not, the coming of Messiah to Israel will be an event of great spiritual as well as international military importance for the whole earth. The blindness of the first-century Jewish contemporaries of Jesus was a result of their unwillingness to accept him as the teacher of righteousness who showed to them in his person and his doctrine the moral perfection of God. If Jesus had been prepared to let them, many would have followed him in rebellion against Rome. This was the kind of Messiah the Jews envisaged; and the prophets certainly gave them much encouragement to look for just such a saviour. So, when Jesus comes again, the Jews will finally recognise in him the national deliverer for whom they have waited so long, and the rest of the world will be brought in subjection to his feet.

But what Israel has yet to learn is the personal side of Messiah's mission – the basis of God's forgiveness, and salvation from sin. If they had only read their scriptures carefully, the Jews might have spared themselves millennia of suffering. It was all there in the promises to Abraham, in the Law of Moses, and in the revelation of the meaning of God's name and the declaration of His moral attributes. It was all there too in Micah's closing words. For, playing on the meaning of his own name, the prophet asked and answered the most searching spiritual question, an understanding of which is the basis of salvation for every man and woman, ourselves included: "*Who is like Yah?*".

And this is the future work of Israel's Messiah: to bring about in the earth that glorification of God's name which will bring in its wake the salvation of man and the fulfilment of all that God has promised since the world began:

"*He will again have compassion on us, and will subdue our iniquities. You* (notice the change to the personal form of address) *will cast all our sins into the depths of the sea. You will give truth to Jacob and mercy to Abraham, which you have sworn to our fathers from days of old.*" (7:19,20)

These are the promises and the visions that Micah held out for the long-term future of God's people – our tomorrow. May it be in that day, when all these things have come to pass, and Micah's mission as a prophet of God is complete, that we might be invited to share with him those glorious things towards which the prophet from Moresheth Gath has helped so many to look with eager anticipation and with joy.

Outline answers to questions

What is the Hope of Israel? (page 25)

1 The promised coming of Shiloh (meaning 'peace') – a king-ruler of the tribe of Judah who will command the people's obedience (Genesis 49:10).

2 Jacob's descendants will be very numerous and his king's kingdom "*shall be exalted*" (Numbers 24:7).

3 The promised king will have a very extensive kingdom (Psalm 72:8).

4 There will be no violence in the earth when everyone alive knows about God (Isaiah 11:9).

5 Israel's future king will be of the line of David and will rule the world successfully with judgement and righteousness (Jeremiah 23:5).

6 The land of Israel will become "*like the garden of Eden*" (Ezekiel 36:35).

7 The faithful dead (like Daniel) will be raised to a new life (Daniel 12:13).

8 "*Living waters*" will flow east and west from Jerusalem, and God will rule over all the world and be universally worshipped (Zechariah 14:8,9).

Questions on part one (page 28)

1.1 In both passages, the hills (mountains) melt before God; God causes an earthquake; fire is poured out; and there is a flood of rushing water.

1.2 It tells us that human beings are not very good at learning from other people's mistakes.

1.3 Micah may well have been a priest or a Levite. He was certainly very well-versed in the teachings of Moses.

1.4 Because it was the physical equivalent of the spiritual promiscuity and unfaithfulness to God involved in idolatry.

1.5 Because the land of Canaan had been promised to Abraham and his children, given to them by God, and divided out to them by Joshua under God's direction. Land was an inheritance which was meant to be kept in the family for ever. Without their allotted land, men and women had nowhere to live, no livelihood, and no status. Taking their land was, in effect, like robbing them of their part in the purpose and kingdom of God.

1.6 God saw to it that the punishment fitted the crime: a) He was devising evil against them (2:3); b) the land they stole from others would be removed from them for ever (2:4,5); and c) they themselves would be utterly destroyed (2:4).

Questions on part two (page 46)

2.1 Micah's three gifts from God were: 1. "*Power*" (3:8), which enabled him to deliver his Divine message in an effective way; 2. "*Justice*", that all-important ability – missing from the rulers of Jerusalem – to discern and uphold the rights of God's people, according to God's righteous laws; 3. "*Might*", the strength that enabled Micah to face opposition and even danger in the service of God.

2.2 They were all greedy for money; and Jesus would have called it serving Mammon (Matthew 6:24). (Mammon was the god of wealth.)

2.3 Because they thought that God would always be with them however they behaved, and that He would never allow His chosen city Jerusalem to be destroyed.

2.4 The people who built the Tower of Babel were scattered by God because they were trying to reach up to heaven by their own efforts. In Micah's vision of the kingdom of God on earth, the scattered nations are brought to Jerusalem to learn the right way to God.

2.5 Because both dew and rain come from God and provide the nourishment needed to make things on the earth grow and thrive.

2.6 Anything that we give our time and interest to more than we do to God, or that matters more to us than He does, whether it's fast cars, fancy houses, the top job, or just a fat bank balance!

Questions on part three (page 57)

3.1 The legal terms in Micah 6:1-3 include: *"plead"*, *"case"*, *"contend with"* (margin: 'bring charges against') and *"testify"*. Such language was appropriate because God was bringing a court-case against His people because they had broken their covenant with Him.

3.2 Because He doesn't want us to give Him external things as sacrifices – what He wants are personal qualities that can be seen in the way that we behave and live.

3.3 Because these are two of the most characteristic attributes of God.

3.4 Both were disappointed with the lack of faithfulness in Israel (verse 1); both felt a sense of isolation among their contemporaries (verses 3,4); both lived at a time of social breakdown (verses 5,6); both put their confidence in God alone (verse 7); both prayed to God and were heard (verse 7); God was a *"light"* to both of them (verses 8,9); and both were mocked by their enemies (verse 10).

3.5 Micah 7:16,17 and Zechariah 14:12-15 taken together suggest that the exercise of God's supernatural power on the nations will produce effects very much like those of nuclear war.

3.6 Salvation from the bondage of sin and death (1 Corinthians 10:1-11).

Supplementary questions (page 62)

1 Idolatrous practices; over-reliance on horses and chariots; working out evil in bed; coveting and stealing fields and houses; stealing clothes off people's backs; making widows and children homeless.

2 By refusing to listen to God's inspired word.

3 By sinning, that is, by failing to come up to God's standard of right behaviour.

4 When God proclaimed His Name to Moses (Exodus 34:5-7), He expressed Himself in terms of His personal moral characteristics. To walk in God's Name, therefore, is to show those same attributes in our daily lives: forgiving sin in others; not retaining our anger; delighting in mercy; showing compassion; and keeping our promises (Micah 7:18,19).

5 Anything that brings spiritual refreshment from God, such as His word, the teaching of Moses, or God's Son (the word made flesh) when he comes again as king.

6 Because they had made idols of them, by relying on them to the point of worshipping them, instead of worshipping God and relying on Him.

7 They wearied God with their sinfulness (Isaiah 43:24).

8 The statutes of Omri were the evil principles that characterised his reign: violence (he killed Tibni to seize the throne of Israel); self-aggrandisement (he founded the city of Samaria); evildoing (*"worse than all who were before him"*); and idolatry. All of these evils are mentioned in 1 Kings 16:21-28, and they had all become common again in the Judah of Micah's day.

9 When they no longer *"continue in unbelief"* (Romans 11:23) or *"blindness"* (verse 25), and are grafted back into their own olive tree at the coming of their Messiah to save *"all Israel"* (both physical and spiritual – verse 26).

10 God promised Abraham nine things:
- a great nation and name (Genesis 12:2,3);
- that he would be a blessing to all families [nations] (12:2,3);
- a seed [descendant(s)] (12:7, etc.);
- a land [the land of Canaan] (12:7, etc.);
- that he would father many nations (17:1-8);
- to make an everlasting covenant with him (17:1-8);
- that Sarah would be the mother of the seed (17:15-21);
- that Ishmael would also be great (17:15-21).
- that his notable seed would conquer the enemy (22:17).

Learning more:

MICAH AND ISAIAH: COMMON LANGUAGE AND SUBJECTS

BY the time Micah's ministry brought him to the nation's capital between 740 and 730 BC, the Jerusalem-based prophet Isaiah had already been prophesying to Judah for more than 15 years. Not surprisingly, given that the same God sent and inspired both prophets, and that they were prophesying in the same contemporary context, there were many points of contact between their prophecies. The table shows some of the many ideas and expressions that were common to both prophets.

Micah	Isaiah	Topic
1:2	34:1	The "earth, and all that is in it"
1:3	26:21	The Lord 'coming out of His place' in judgement
1:8	43:20	Jackals and ostriches
1:9-16	10:28-32	The advance of the Assyrian army
1:16	3:24	Baldness to replace ornate hair
2:1,2	5:8	Woe to those who covet and steal other people's fields
2:3	2:11	Judgement to come on the haughty
2:6	30:9,10	False prophets
2:11	28:7	Drunken prophets
2:12	10:20	The promise of a returning remnant
2:13	52:12	God's people going out *"with the Lord at their head"*
3:1,2	1:17,23	Corruption of justice and bribery in the magistrates' courts

Micah	Isaiah	Topic
3:4	8:17	God hiding His face from His people
3:5-7	29:9-12	No visions from God for the false prophets
3:8	58:1	"To declare to Jacob his transgression"
3:11	48:2	Leaning complacently on the Lord
3:11	7:14	'Is not the Lord among us?' / Immanuel ('God with us')
4:1-3	2:2-4	The "mountain of the LORD's house" (Jerusalem) becomes the centre of world government
4:4	36:16	The Rabshakeh quotes Micah's 'vine and fig tree' promise!
4:6	56:8	God will "gather the outcasts"
4:6,7	1:26,27; 24:23	God's rule in Zion over the returning captives
4:9	13:8	"Pangs have seized you like a woman in labour"
4:10	39:6	Babylonian captivity foretold for the daughter of Zion
4:13	41:15	Zion (ultimately) to thresh her enemies
5:2-4	7:14	The birth of the Messiah-child
5:4	40:11	A promise of the Shepherd-king of Israel
5:4	30:27	"the name of the LORD"
5:5	9:6	Messiah: the (Prince of) peace promised
5:10	31:1	A misplaced confidence in horses and chariots
5:12-14	2:6-9	Soothsayers, horses, chariots and idols to be destroyed
5:13	2:8	"You shall no more worship the work of your hands"
6:1-16	1:2-20	God's court case against His people
6:2	43:26	The Lord "contends" with Israel

Micah	Isaiah	Topic
6:3	43:22	God's people weary of Him
6:6-8	1:11-17	The morality that God requires of His people
6:9-12	1:21-23	Jerusalem full of immorality, violence, corruption and theft
7:2	57:1	No good or faithful men left
7:4	21:6	The prophet as "watchman"
7:7	8:17	Waiting patiently for God
7:10	10:6	Trampled down like mud in the streets
7:12	11:11	God bringing back His captives from Assyria "in that day"
7:16	26:11	The nations to be ashamed when they see God's might exercised on behalf of Israel
7:17	65:25	Licking dust like a serpent in the presence of the Lord

Further reading

THERE is no shortage of commentaries on Micah; but virtually all of them (old and new alike) are spoiled in varying degrees by the unhelpful and often highly speculative views of the so-called Higher Criticism, which treats the Bible as if it were no more than a work of human literature. As far as the author is aware, this book is the first full-length study of Micah's prophecy written by a Christadelphian; and the view adopted here is that the whole of Micah as we now have it was edited in the eighth-century BC by Micah himself, under the direct inspiration of God, as the prophet categorically states (3:8).

Other books that take the same view of the Divine inspiration of Micah, and which can therefore be recommended as helps to a reliable understanding of the prophet's mission and message, include:

- Fred Pearce, *From Hosea to Zephaniah: Studies in the Minor Prophets before the Exile* (Birmingham, The Christadelphian, 1979). Chapter 8 (pages 128-156) is a self-contained study of Micah by a respected Christadelphian writer for whom the Minor Prophets represented a long-term personal interest.

- Harry Whittaker, *Hezekiah the Great* (Birmingham, The Christadelphian, 1985). Published in a single volume together with *The Songs of Degrees*, by George Booker, this book is full of valuable and surprising insights into the life and times of one of Judah's most important kings, in whose reign Micah prophesied.

- Michael Ashton, *Chronicles of the Kings* (Birmingham, The Christadelphian, 2003). Chapters 26 and 27 (pages 177-191) are a succinct and extremely helpful guide to the background of Micah's life and times.

Among the modern commentaries on Micah, the most useful (and perhaps the least unreliable) is Bruce Waltke's *Micah: an Introduction and Commentary* (Leicester: Inter-Varsity Press, 1988), while the translation of Micah published by J.B. Phillips (*Four prophets ... a Modern Translation from the Hebrew* (London: Bles, 1963)) makes the prophecy very readable by putting it into verse-form.

Older works on Micah consulted by the author, and found of some value, include:

- R.F. Horton, *Micah: Introduction and Revised Version, with annotations* (London, The Caxton Publishing Company, about 1910). [The Century Bible Commentary]

- T.K. Cheyne, *Micah, with notes and introduction* (Cambridge, University Press, 1891). [The Cambridge Bible for Schools and Colleges]

- E.B. Pusey, *The Minor Prophets* (Oxford, Parker, 1860).